T0326272

CRITICAL APPROACHES
VOL. 1
THE WORKS OF CHIN CE

Edited by
Irene Marques

[Ph.D., Comparative Literature]
Department of Liberal Studies
Ontario College of Arts and
Design, Canada

HANDEL
Library of African Writing

CRITICAL APPROACHES Vol. 1
The Works of Chin Ce

Irene Marques [Ed.]

World-Wide Web:
 Handel Books Ltd.
http://www.hbooknetworks.com

Front and Back Cover: *African Books Network*

Published by
The African Books Network
Handel Books Limited
6/9 Handel Avenue
AI EBS Nigeria WA
Email: handelbook@yahoo.co.uk

Marketing and Distribution in the U.S. UK,
Europe, N. America (US and Canada),
and Commonwealth countries outside Africa by
African Books Collective Ltd.
PO Box 721
Oxford OX1 9EN
UK
Email: orders@africanbookscollective.com

ISBN:978-9-7835-0344-0

A Handel Book Publication

Contents

Introduction

Nigeria's Chin Ce is one of the younger stream of writers from Africa who has his talents spread across the genres. Author of several works of fiction, poetry and seminal essays on literature, Ce evokes a deeper sense of personal duty and mutual friendships while dwelling upon highly imaginative constructs that challenge the reader to such positive participation in a world-constant of changing realities.

Chin Ce was born of Igbo parents south east of Nigeria, and is said to belong to the "(Nigerian civil) war generation" in a somewhat local manner of expression. Educated at Calabar and trained as a journalist, he was not long in exercising the literary skills that earnestly inspired his reading and research projects in Nigeria and Ghana.

The publication of *An African Eclipse* in 1992 introduced Chin Ce as a political writer of profound awareness of national and continental history. However, unlike his fellows of the younger stream of writers from Africa also influenced by the political and social conditions of their nations, Ce's art was soon to carve its own stamp of identity by his eclectic and interdisciplinary fusion of perspectives which lend his works deeper and wider significance.

Chin Ce's oeuvres here under study include his well known fictions, *Children of Koloko* [2001], *Gamji College* [2002] and poetry, *An African Eclipse* [1992]. The three have been subjects of critical commentaries on modern Nigerian (read African) experiments in nation-state building by few critics of African literature. Attempts have also been made to give Chin Ce's other works, *The Visitor* [2004] (fiction) and *Full Moon* [2001] (poetry) as much critical attention here as his *Millennial* [2005] collection of poems. These papers taken as an overview reveal, as is the aim of this volume, the ideals, craft and vision of Chin Ce's fictional preoccupation in recent times.

As a writer living in a society whose peculiar continental dilemmas and propositions are encysted by still extant historical destiny, Ce is often confronted with the problem of artistic interpretation of these dilemmas, to imbue a sense of individual and collective meaning to the apathy and atrophy of the younger African generation to which he belongs.

It was initially the aim of this book to update some of the significant responses and approaches to the works of this self-effacing African writer as a journal supplement where the larger credit goes to contributors and other publishing facilitators interested and committed to providing and sustaining a regular stream of online and printed discourses on contemporary African literatures and cultures where mainstream local publishing has been virtually apathetic. Today with the involvement of Handel Books, we can present a total of 10 book chapters on Ce's works as only a mild testimony to the wider interest and acceptance which the Nigerian writer might continue to generate among scholars of African literature around the world.

IM

 Overviews

1

Critical Approaches

TO THE WORKS OF CHIN CE

Irene Marques

CHILDREN OF KOLOKO: *Too Much Newness*

In her essay "Educating the Child with Camara Laye's *The Dark Child* and Chin Ce's *Children of Koloko*" DM Toko provides in-depth and sound comparative discourse of the education given to the protagonists of Camara Laye's *The Dark Child* and Chin Ce's *Children of Koloko*. Despite the fact that the two novels depict colonial and post-colonial societies respectively, they do in many ways bring to debate the same issue: how to positively imprint African cultural values on the minds of youngsters, especially in the face of constant interference of exogenic values.

With its emphasis on community, family, as well as the natural and spiritual world, and the relationality between all of these, the African traditional community teaches the child to respect others and otherness, and to also show responsibility for his/her actions – actions that may affect the balance of the community. By showing how the main protagonists of both works become strong and balanced individuals precisely because they are anchored in African conventional wisdom and cultural values, Toko demonstrates that

Chin Ce and Camara Laye believe in the importance of Africa's culture as a springboard for 'real' growth and success of the continent. By raising children to believe and respect the positive aspects of African conventional wisdoms, it is then possible to have balanced and fulfilled humans beings –beings who know how to find steadiness, even in the face of violent sea waves, in short, adults who are spiritually, psychologically and communally grounded and do not fall into utter madness like Dickie does in *Children of Koloko*. As Toko argues, both Laye's and Ce's novels seem to favour an education that will take into account traditional African values, while at the same time welcoming western values which will contribute to the amelioration of the lives of African peoples. The creation of a hybrid way, or a "middle course" (11) as Amanda Grants might rather say, is what both Laye and Ce seem to be advocating for in their respective novels. After all, how can one really know the weather of today, and think about the sun of tomorrow, if one cannot remember the suns and rains of yesterday?

Jonas Cope and Kay Chester use the language-relativist[1] approach in their critique of Toni Morrison's *Beloved* and Chin Ce's *Children of Koloko*. The authors demonstrate how language is a fundamental tool to 'say' the being it wants and needs to say: to 'say' the African-American slave or the unstable and unsure postcolonial subject of Nigeria. Is it then a question of "Stealing the White Man's Weapon or Forging One's Own?" they ask. Cope and Chester illustrate how the speaking of a language is a complicated and multifaceted affair. Speaking a language that is different from the language of the white master is, for the characters of *Beloved*, a socio-political, ontological and spiritual gesture –a gesture that produces a sense of identity, cohesion and discovery for most Black Americans. Speaking a language that the master cannot understand is thus a way to defend the Self against the Other, a way to create or recreate that very Self. Initially this Self needs to be the Antithesis of the master's Thesis, yes, only because the Thesis is too alienating, too reductive, where the Other is not, cannot, be part of the Self, for the Self in his blindness, fails to see outside His lens. But to speak and forge a language that not even the Black-American slave can understand can also be highly liberating for he and she who utter it for the very first time, for when language "overstands"[2] as the Rastafarians will say, then we understand: You and I, Him and Her, are able to travel beyond the stagnant poverty often enforced by linguistic classifications and enter the divine, the realm where seeing in fact is being. Many poets and writers have already affirmed this conviction, and so have the Buddhists[3]. And so has Morrison, and quite beautifully in *Beloved*.

But can we say that that 'Beloved' language is also the language of *Children of Koloko*? Chin Ce's story-collection seems to be a language of loss, a language of confusion, rather than the language of liberation, or of findings. Ce's characters inhabit a postcolonial world where greed, corruption, despair and deprecation for African traditional values seem to prevail –a world where youths are not learning from the elaborate, complex and literary oral traditions that once were vibrating sounds, live powerful metaphors, constantly caressing and nourishing the minds of the youths. The speech "parroted" by Ce's characters seems poor, colloquial and spiritually devoid: just like their lives. By displaying this poor speech, Chin Ce's seems to be pointing the finger and saying: "Look at how poor we have become…" He seems to be mourning that *Beloved* language of the Nigerian (and African) past. But can that language be recovered, recreated? Can we say that the poor dwellers of *Children of Koloko* are the only "parrots" of the contemporary world? Have you paid attention to the language that the Western youths tend to speak? Too much television perhaps and all the other technological advances… And not enough stories told by the fireplace, those stories intertwined

13

with the flickering mystery of the yellow and red flames to nourish the soul... Too much newness and what we might need is the old reawakened.

GAMJI COLLEGE: 'Diagnostician of State'

In her essay "Chin Ce and the Postcolonial Dialogue of Gamji College" Gloria Emezue offers a comparison between Chin Ce's *Gamji College* and some of Achebe's novels. Emezue argues that *Gamji College*, with Ce's other fictions and some of his early poetry in general, revolves around three fundamental precepts: "the commitment to and awareness of [the author's] environment, the testing of its notions on the scale of general communal good and past history, and the artiste's response to this test being the rejection of unwholesome, even if popular paradigms that paralyse or constrain genuine social transformation"(90). She rightly maintains that there is in Ce's work a concern with dialogue, a preoccupation to uncover the behaviours of postcolonial Nigerian subjects, an attempt to show the reader the miserable state of affairs of the Nigerian post-colonial nation, and also, an attempt to devise another way of being, of seeing, of understanding, of questioning that could lead to a better and more realized nation. Like in *An African Eclipse*, or in some of Chin Ce's other works, the narrative/authorial voice does not merely want to show the reader what is wrong, but also why things are wrong and what might constitute a better alternative. The writer wants to engage in the displaying of history for the understanding of that very history is crucial if favourable change is to occur. The post-colonial subject cannot, or should not, disregard history – pre, colonial, and postcolonial history – for it is the very understanding of that history, and the dynamics between pre, colonial and postcolonial societies that will allow him/her to create a nation in a truer sense of the word. A nation that will take into account pre, colonial and post colonial socio-political dynamics is an informed nation, a richer nation, a conscientious nation.

The relationship between past, present and future is of extreme importance, thus the need for education – the writer is the educator, the one who allows for transhistorical, transpersonal, and even transfictional dialogue to take place. The writer allows for dialogue between characters and also dialogue between characters and readers. Such multiple dialogues permit a more wholesome understanding of the troubles of the post-colonial nation via constant direct or indirect expositions of socio-historical realities. The writer exposes the different situations and the different characters in such a fashion that the reader can see him/herself reflected in them, allowing for self-recognition and thus 'conscientialization' – the first step to positive action. The one who interacts inside the fiction (the character) and the one who reads that fiction (the reader) learns from either directly experiencing, observing or reflecting about the misery, confusion, wise and unwise decision-making of the 'players' of what comes across as a clearly unhealthy nation. Just like Jerry and Tai (*Gamji College*) seem to learn from observing the miseries of others, the reader too can learn from the display of mostly decadent situations, actions and poor or misinformed ways of thinking and perceiving reality.

The very discussion between the youths in the section "The Bottle" allows for the reader and the characters to learn or reflect upon what is happening to them. The inebriated state of the characters allows for a discussion that is mostly nonsensical and which borders upon the psychotic. But it might be precisely because of the nature of this discussion that both readers and (maybe less) characters are able to realize how things are out of control, 'out' of humanity, in sheer dis-humanity, absurd in a widened sense of the term, and the reasons why that might be. For instance, the youth Milord, in his state of utter drunkenness has a hazy (confused) vision of himself as someone inserted in history, be it past or future. The questions Ce seems to be asking are: How does one maintain oneself adequately sober (informed and aware) so that one is capable of seeing oneself as an agent that is inserted in history, and consequently, also as an agent capable of making, and changing that very history? How do we have a clear, holistic and interdynamical understanding of history so that we can then pave the way for a more genuine and ethical society?

We can see therefore in Ce's works that the mirror effect is present in various ways: the mirror of history via the use of overt or covert inter-dynamic historical representations and the mirror of character-to-character or character-to-reader. This multi-dimensional didactic mirror is a narrative technique of major importance in *Gamji College*, and also in several of Ce's other fictional or poetic works. By making use of this mirror –by putting the malaises on display and by showing the many agents, and trans-historical and socio-religio-politico 'agencies' that are making the society the putrid pit it is– the writer, like the doctor, is writing a complete and thorough chart, thus becoming what Coetzee calls "the medical diagnostician of the state" (qtd. in Hamilton 98). In a manner similar to Michel Foucault, the writer becomes the intellectual whose main responsibility is to show the many dynamics that are 'constituting' us, playing us, the dynamics that are making us blind agents or subjects who obey without reflection, without questioning –without careful dissection of the vast trans-historical institutional beast and its many circular and cavernous effects[4]. But, and like any good doctor, and perhaps in a more prescriptive manner than Foucault, who has described himself as non-prescriptive (*Power* 240), it seems that Ce does more than diagnose or describe: he prescribes, he offers a cure, or at least the beginning of a cure. And that cure, or the beginning of that cure, lies in showing that a constant dialogue between past, present and future is the fundamental recipe for success, the fundamental recipe for a more accomplished postcolonial nation.

In 'Pedagogy of Disillusionment: The Case of Ferdinand Oyono's *The Old Man and the Medal* and Chin Ce's *Gamji College*' Kenneth Usongo suggests that the self-realization of his state of subjugation by the oppressed in Oyono's *The Old Man and the Medal* is the first step towards the eradication of colonial oppression and the rebuilding of Afro-centred cultural pride and success. The author shows us how the protagonist of the novel, Meka, gradually realizes that he is not much more than a necessary broker, or a make-believe agent, between the French colonial master and the local Cameroonian people, an agent that helps the French spread their power and culture locally thus nullifying African values, yet one who gains no real power in the process. Meka starts off with a naïve expectation about the benefits that such an alliance with the colonial master will bring him, then moves onto all the anxieties, uncertainties and confusion about his place and value as a 'real' subject within the unequal colonial dichotomy of Self/Other, only to finally reach the point of disillusion. This point of disillusion is crucial for the oppressed subjects under consideration in Oyono's novel since it reveals to them the real intention of the colonizer, thus making them aware of the necessity to act and take charge of their lives. In that sense Oyono's novel is pedagogic as Usongo asserts in the very title of his article.

In a similar way, Chin Ce's collection of stories, *Gamji College*, Usongo further avers, mirrors the stages of expectations, dream fragmentations and disillusionment in its three sections: "The Cross," "The Bottle," and "The Gun". *Gamji College* shows how the death of direct European colonialism did not end economical and cultural imperialism, oppression, violence and disappointment since the colonial authorities were replaced with neo-colonial figures that perpetuate the cycle of mal-governance and become obsessed with material wealth and imitation of Western values, often discarding African values of brotherhood and communalism. Christian religion appears as the favourite sister of the state, creating a despotic state-nation where the president, *à la façon* of the opulent French King Louis the XIV, impersonates God, imposing his will and controlling all the mechanisms to ensure his throne. *Gamji College* is therefore the metaphor for the Nigerian (and African) post-colonial messy state-nation, that *beast* that cannot stop being a *beast*, that state that yearns to become a nation.

It is the likes of young Tai and Jerry who, in their utter disillusionment, find it necessary to reject the greed, corruption, group favouritism, blind religious fanaticism and violent nihilism of their society. They do so by asserting their view and position or by removing themselves from certain situations or from the company of people who remind them of their own disillusion. In a way, the people they interact with function as mirrors showing them what they themselves have or can become, but also what they do not want to become. The ugliness of those mirrors has a positive effect on them: it reminds them of the dreams they might have or the dreams they once had and the goals they still want to realize. It is the disenchantment of others, constantly being reflected back at them, that propels them to resist the trend of moral decay, greed and nihilism. Thus they are the ones who give us hope, hope that the nation will be one day, hope that the beautiful one, the true African Princess, will shine forth. For now though she seems to be only pulsating under Bisi's heavy artificial mascara and meditated catwalk.

THE VISITOR : *New States of Being*

In his reading of *The Visitor*, Chin Ce's full-length and --most complex– novel, Okuyade Ogaga illustrates how Ce uses a mixture of realist, modernist and Africanist narrative techniques to create a unique novel –a novel that mixes western narrative methods with

African traditions of storytelling. In a fashion similar to modernist writers, Ce weaves a narrative where truth and being, their unstable, indefinable and ever-changing nature, and the multiplicity of voice figure as the foundation of his novelistic poetics. By so doing Ce is able to demonstrate the 'hybrid' and changing nature of many African post-colonial nations

We are privy to nations whose identity oscillates between Africanness and Westernness, between embracing African values and Western ones, between epistemologies that value reason and unidimensionality and those that esteem mystical, unconscious and holistic dimensions of life's apprehension.

As in many of the other woks produced by Ce, the mystical dimension is presented to us as the most complete for it allows us to be in a grander way. It allows us to exit the smallness of the corrupt world of Nigeria, where gun violence, bribery, and moral decay are regrettably too frequent and do prevent us from seeing. *The Visitor* allows us to connect past, present and future, to become aware of ourselves in a broader manner, to travel through the world of the ancestors or the spirit plane, where being is, where the world is no longer a market place as the Igbo saying, placed at the beginning of Ce's novel foretells, but rather a home – that home where the inhabitants are no longer visitors but permanent dwellers instead. They are dwellers who, through a cross-temporal and cross-conscious didactic voyage, or a type of circular osmosis, can see outside of themselves only to see more deeply into themselves, and also into others.

These dwellers – Grandad, Uzi, Adaku, etc.– with whom we get to be intimate in that 'maze' that is *The Visitor*, attain a state of being that brings about a profound and blissful transcendental completeness and connectedness. By seeing into the life of these dwellers through their alternate states of existence and consciousness, and through the rich and poetic imagery evoked by Ce, we the readers, are also pulled into their osmotic state, and are indeed reminded of an alternate existence, one that we can call sublime.

When we compare that sedate and grandly evolved existence to the bare and poor 'state of being' of the Nigerian contemporary society, and, more broadly, to many contemporary societies, we almost want to cry, or emit a sigh – that sigh of profound yearning.

AN AFRICAN ECLIPSE: '*The Chain of Ignorance'*

G.A.R Hamilton's study of Ce's collection of poetry *An African Eclipse* offers an alternative and profound view for the socio-political reformation of Nigeria necessitating its reissue in this volume. Drawing mainly on the works of Jean-Paul Sartre, Gilles Deleuze and Chinua Achebe, Hamilton demonstrates how *An African Eclipse* is a work that aims at much more than pointing the finger at the moral and ethical flaws of post-independence political leaders--much more than the mere displaying of the socio-political arena of a very troubled nation.

By depicting the many psychosocial, ethnic and environmental miseries that have afflicted post-colonial Nigeria and by showing how such miseries are in many ways a result of what can be termed an individualistic, if not ignorant, ontology, Ce's poetry moves to the displaying of a non-personal Life force, presenting it as the solution to the general inertia affecting Nigeria. The poet paints this non-personal Life force, which can also be named the Soul, or the Social or Collective Ethics, as being oriented by the common good and not by the individual and egoistic desires of the single mind or minority group. For such ontological ethics of the collective to triumph it is necessary that each individual sees him/herself as a responsible agent, an able being capable of thinking outside that which is fed to him/her by the political corrupt machinery. The individual being must think, learn, become able, and break the chains of ignorance so that he/she can then become a reliable and capable agent, the one who can be the foundation of a Social-collective Ethics and of a new healthier Nigerian nation. There is, as Hamilton points out, a need to move from the State-organized ontologies into individual thinking, which will then become the basis of a renewed collective ontology.

Thus the poet of *An African Eclipse* also becomes a critic of the aggressive drive of modernization, capitalism and imperialism that permeates Nigeria with its rampant exploitation of natural resources disregarding the need for preservation of the Nigerian land, and its disinterest for a more equal distribution of resources. This aggressive drive and individualistic trend does not give enough consideration to the traditional values of community and inter-help and has little or no regard for nature, in other words, it shows minimal regard for what might be termed as a hermeneutics of holism – the positive values of the forefathers and foremothers who lived before our times. The new class of politicians and nation 'teachers' are not exemplary teachers, or, they are not teachers at all. They do not know how, or care, to teach their children (the citizens of Nigeria) because they constitute bad examples of governance and display the un-ethical characteristics of individualism, greed, corruption, ignorance, and psychological and physical violence.

In a fashion similar to many other politically conscious African writers, Ce becomes the teacher himself. In the absence of capable politicians who can teach or govern a nation ethically, the writer/poet becomes "the medical diagnostician of the state" (98), Hamilton points out, directly quoting J. M. Coetzee. As the conscientious "diagnostician," the writer/poet shows people how things work in the wretched state but also how they ought to work in a state genuinely concerned with the welfare of its people.

Through his poetry, Ce tries to communicate with the reader by painting the present and past history of Nigeria and also by envisaging a future when things might be different when we might be "in the season of another [better] life" as the last poem of the collection points to. The poet is always careful to tell the reader to think and reflect back into history, to remember good and bad, to remember poverty and wealth, to "watch over the earth" so that the "ambitions that [may] lurk in the dark corners /of the mind" (58) might not take over, causing us to fall again into the darkness on the *African Eclipse*. This dialogue between present, past and future is fundamental for it serves to illustrate the intrinsic relationship that exists between the different temporal realities, thus showing the reader to learn from what has happened.

Chin Ce is therefore a didactic poet, emphasising the importance of knowing history well –what happened; how, why, or who was involved; or how all these play into the current state of affairs, and so forth. Only by being aware of the historical realities can the present Nigerian post-colonial subject emerge stronger, conscientious and realized, which in turn will allow for the surging of a new, stronger and reformed nation. There is in *An African Eclipse* an intimate camaraderie between the reader and the poetic subject. This intimate camaraderie further points to Ce's emphasis on the 'we', the Collective and Social Ethics where reader and writer become agents involved in the same battle. As Hamilton contends, the writer is no longer the one "who simply represents experience through writing, which is to say a writer "*for* or *on the behalf of*" (113). Instead, the writer becomes

> [A]n inextricable element of the people, who, in refusing to simply represent personal experiences, creates non-preexistent relations between poets, readers, and the process of becoming revolutionary, in order to demonstrate new possibilities of Life – new ways of

living within Nigeria. (113)

It is the "I" and the "You" that can watch over the earth, over the nation. It is the "I/poet" and the "You/reader" that have the power to move away from the State-organized ontologies and into the individual, and then collectively organized ontologies, where the social welfare of the collectivity is at the forefront. Through such interrogation and awareness of oneself and the world, it is then possible to move into ethically and collective oriented responsible ways of being.

As in other of his works, there is in *An African Eclipse* an emphasis by Chin Ce on personal engagement, an integrative cognizance and concern for the wellbeing of others and otherness –be it human, physical or transcendental entities – and an exhibiting of the interrelationship between present, past and future. Humans appear as multidimensional entities that are tied with the larger spatio-temporal and spiritual realities and therefore need to tap into those realities if they are to attain fecundity and fulfilment both as individuals and citizens of a true nation-state. As the poet says: "Only the soul /like dynamite /can burst the chain of ignorance" (45). *An African Eclipse* is thus a work that favours and calls for an ontology of holism and cooperation in the most varied sense of these terms.

One may further compare Chin Ce's philosophy or ethics of writing, his preoccupation with the Other, and his appreciation for fluid epistemologies, with Emmanuel Lévinas's ethical concerns. Like Ce, the Lithuanian-French philosopher, Lévinas, seems concerned with the mystical, fluid and poetic apprehension of life, and with the fundamental importance of an inter-relational ontology, the fundamental importance of the relationship between Self and Other, Self and Otherness. Both present the spiritual look, or the Soul as Ce might call it, as the method capable of overcoming restrictions, nihilistic categories and reductive subjectifications and objectifications that are the base of much distress and exploitation of humans by humans, of nature by humans. When reading Chin Ce, one can easily think of Lévinas's fascinating, if not enigmatic work, *Totality and Infinity* or even *Time and Other*. An in-depth and comparative study between the two authors will very likely constitute an interesting cross-cultural project.

FULL MOON: Mind, Nature and Cosmos

In his essay, "'Closer to Wordsworth': Nature and Pain in Chin Ce's Full Moon poems", Kola Eke reasons that Chin Ce's poetry is intrinsically animistic and romantic in a manner reminiscent of both William Wordsworth, and Leopold Senghor, one of the finest African poets of the Négritude movement. "With Chin Ce, nature and human mind are inseparable" (193), says Eke. One could easily add in an inflated metaphor: In Ce's poetry mind and nature are brother and sister, son and mother, wave and sea, reflector and reflected.

Chin Ce's poetry collection, *Full Moon,* is indeed full –full in the sense that it shows the deep relationship that exists between the state of the poet's mind and the state of his natural surroundings. The poet's mind becomes the mind of the nature, or even more, the mind of the cosmos, the mind of the beyond. To satisfy a visceral anthropomorphic and transcendental need, the mind of the poetic subject becomes the very being of nature, or the very being of the universe at large, with rivers and trees, boats and harmattan(s), suns and moons, clouds and skies (…) becoming mirrors of the deep sensibilities and desires of the poet, of his need to travel through the confines of time, space and material reality. The poet's fundamental, quasi-organic need (or requirement) is not just to merge with the terrestrial; it is also to merge with the extraterrestrial.

In Chin Ce's poetry, nature is not always the nice princess that can bring solace to the mind of the poet. Nature often shows how violent it can be, as violent perhaps as some tyrannical and corrupt governors of past or current Nigeria as the poem "The Call" alludes to:

> Because I have seen how long lies the road
> Beyond the setting minds of men
>
> Because I looked past the hungers of today
> And drank some deep beyond the doctrines
>
> I can look the raving tyrant in the eye
> And see the yawning emptiness of his glare...
> (15)

It is precisely because the poet has seen "beyond the setting minds of men," "looked past the hungers of today" and "see[n] the yawning emptiness of [the tyrant's] glare" that he can exit his smallness, and the smallness and oppressive nature of his socio-political and material milieu and travel. His travelling allows him to meet the Soul, whose call he has heard:

> Because I have heard the call of the soul
> That haunts my wild and restless mind
>
> I shall forge along to build my dream
> On the hills beyond the rising sun (15)

Our poetic speaker is a "Journey man," as he points out in another poem, "a traveller of the High way," "the dream of silent night" (18), that "silent night" where the noise, the worries and the littleness of this world are annihilated or suspended. His ability to travel spiritually via what could be called the transit of poetic metaphor is what makes him a larger ontological being as illustrated in the capitalized poem "I AM" (16). His being becomes divine, cosmical, far exceeding the confines of the physical sphere.

Ce's poetry is profoundly beautiful and easy to the eye and to the mind. His language is generally not obscure; it possesses a pristine transparency that aligns itself with the poet's need to merge with the larger self. And furthermore, because of its foremost levity, it permits the reader to also share in the pleasure of the extra-terrestrial voyage that is the mind of the poet and enjoy, enjoy.... As Wordsworth would say himself: "The Poet, singing a song in which all human beings join with him, rejoices in the presence of truth as our visible friend and hourly companion" (259).

Thus Chin Ce's poetry, like all powerful poetry, is a divine call, a profound yearning for wholeness in a world that has become too acquainted with the smallness of dissected disconnected particles. Ce's poetry is circular and round like the Moon when it is Full. Or like the revolving call of the wolf, who in his desperate and lonely night calls the 'lover' that he has lost and misses dearly. If the characters of *Children of Koloko* speak the language of loss, confusion and spiritual decadence, the shamanistic speaker of *Full Moon* in a manner suggestive of *Beloved*, utters the language of discoveries, enlightenment and transcendence.

MILLENNIAL Disappointments and Renewals

In a brief statement on *Millennial*, Chin Ce's third volume of poetry, Charles Smith notes that the poet-persona, having toured his neighbour-nations, returns to native land "with his usual ribaldry at the 'buffoonery of the millennium' which political leaders and heads of Nigeria represent" (202). *Millennial* is thus full of personal disappointments. The haunting dirge tenor of most recent poetry from Africa still persists through a new craft that upholds the making of new friendships through journeys of the millennial dawn. It is however contended that this is a good indication that the personal introversion of the *Millennial* poems does not obscure the social commitment of Chin Ce's last collection of poetry. Smith declares:

Millennial will prove to be Chin Ce's most readable and intensely personal poetry, flowing with a maturity of craft that echoes previous sentiments while yet seeking those new 'vistas of illumination' that have become the recurring framework for the interpretation or appreciation of the works of Chin Ce. (204)

Yet, despite of all the millennial disappointments, the question that remains in *Millennial* is the question that permeates most, if not all, of Chin Ce's works: how to reach the 'season of another life'? And this question is reiterated in the poem "Millennial" once more as a powerful call to consciousness and awareness. The poem brings about, and in a profoundly mourning tone, the need to reform the individual and collectivity. It refers to that constant and haunting sentiment of the desire of the human soul, a soul that does not and must not leave the poet or the reader. The poem comes across as a call to not forget, a call to not let go –it is a call for the recuperation of ecological and human dignity, unity and higher awareness, a call for "God and Country" (197) as Smith puts it. This call, if heard and followed, is what will save the Nigerian citizen and allow him/her to attain full *beingness*, a being concerned with and in touch with others – the human collectivity– but also with otherness: the earthly/ecological and spiritual collectivity. The awareness of these collectivities or entities will pave the way for that most waited and yearned for nation – the nation in the 'season of another life':

> Sometimes you find me
> like a lone egret
> perched on some withered
> height. (58)

Millennial is a reminder that the time of the positive prophecy, the 'beautiful one', has not yet arrived:

...wondering what
became of us
that can no longer see
with eyes that look in another;

and the smile that stretches
far and deep
connecting souls. (58)

But it is also a reminder that that prophecy, that beautiful, lives in each of us, and it is as old perhaps as the human spirit; it is millenary, and it pounds in our hearts, it hounds us continuously, sometimes so much so, that You and I fall into convulsive crying, even though we might not consciously know the reason:

. . . .
Let not the world
be a limpid cataract
hounding its connoisseurs
through but hollow destinies. (61)

"Millennial" makes us think about that Beautiful confined to the minor hidden realms of ourselves, and it does so in a profoundly sad mournful manner, bringing to us feelings of deep regret, yearning and perhaps even tears. Yet, those very feelings evoked by the poem, awaken in us the renewed desire to uncover that very Beautiful. Let the world not be a limpid cataract. Let it BE. Because it hurts so much as it is. Here then is an adequate or appropriate index to our critical appreciation of the oeuvres of Chin Ce, a writer who, in most or all the opinions may yet remain the most significant voice of twenty-first century Nigerian and African writing.

NOTES

[1]Generally speaking language relativism refers to the idea that language molds the way we see reality and ourselves. Different languages emerge out of different socio-cultural, physical, ontological and epistemological environments and therefore each language will communicate something different. By creating new ways of communicating, the African-American slave is evading the white master's way of thinking, seeing, and ultimately, the power dynamics and discriminatory dichotomies that exist within the slave/master society. A new language signifies the negation of the white man's worldview, a negation of his values, legitimacy to power and superiority, it constitutes an annihilation of his claims. In a similar fashion, *écriture féminine* or *écriture au féminin* (feminine writing) as defined for instance by the French Hélène Cixous or the French Canadian France Théoret respectively, also evades the patriarchal power networks by refusing to obey conventional writings mechanisms and allowing the 'non-rational' intelligences to speak. For further discussions on the subject of language relativism, and *écriture féminine* or *écriture au féminin* see Ngũgĩ's *Decolonizing the Mind*, Whorf's *Language, Thought, and Reality*, Cixous's *La jeune née* and Théoret's *Entre raison et déraison,* respectively.

[2]For further discussions on the concepts of "overstanding" and "dread talk" see Velma Pollard's book *Dread Talk: The Language of Rastafarians*, J. Edward Chamberlin's *Come Back to Me My Language* and also my own article "Mia Couto and the Holistic Choric Self: Recreating the Broken Cosmic Order (Or: Relearning the Song that Truly Speaks...)" in *JALC* no. 4. This concept of "dread talk" is of course related to the concept of language relativism as referred to above (note 1) –at least in the sense that the oppressed group (the slave or the woman) find it necessary to forge their own *sui generis* language to evade the oppressive systems that operate within their society or to access a mystical/non-man's 'land' that circumvents discriminatory categories.

[3]See for example Lispector's *Água Viva* and *A Hora da Estrela*, and

29

Suzuki's *The Essentials of Zen Buddhism*.

[4]For an understanding of Foucault's thinking and his discussion on the construction of power, knowledge, truth and the 'making' of the subject via the various historical agents see *Power: Essential Works of Foucault 1954-1984*. See also *The Archaeology of Knowledge* and *The History of Sexuality*.

WORKS CITED

Ce, Chin. *An African Eclipse*. Enugu: Handel Books, 2000.

___. *Children of Koloko*. Enugu: Handel Books, 2001.

___. *Full Moon*. Enugu: Handel Books, 1992.

___. *Gamji College*. Enugu: Handel Books, 2002.

___. *Millennial*. Enugu: Handel Books, 2005.

___. *The Visitor*. Enugu: Handel Books, 2004.

Chamberlin, J. Edward. *Come Back to Me My Language: Poetry and the West Indies*. Urbana: University of Illinois P, 1993.

Cixous, Hélène and Catherine Clément. *La jeune née*. Paris: Union générale d'éditions, 1975.

Cope, Jonas and Kay Chester. "Stealing the White Man's Weapon or Forging One's Own? African and African-American English in Ce's *Children of Koloko* and Morrison's *Beloved*." *Critical Supplement: The Works of Chin Ce*. IRCALC, 2007. 63-86.

Eke, Kola. "'Closer to Wordsworth': Nature and Pain in Chin Ce's Full Moon poems." *Critical Supplement: The Works of Chin Ce*. IRCALC, 2007. 185-196.

Emezue, MT Gloria. "Chin Ce and The Postcolonial Dialogue of *Gamji College*." *Critical Supplement: The Works of Chin Ce*. IRCALC, 2007. 87-110.

Foucault, Michel. *Power: Essential Works of Foucault 1954-1984: Vol. 3*. Ed. James D. Faubion, Trans. Robert Hurley And Others. New York: The New Press, 2000.

___. *The Archaeology of Knowledge & The Discourse on Language*.

Trans. A. M. Sheridan Smith. New York: Pantheon Books, 1972.

_ _ _. *The History of Sexuality: An Introduction-Vol 1*. Trans. Robert Hurley. New York: Vintage Books, 1990.

Grants, Amanda. "Memory, Transition and Dialogue: The Cyclic Order of Chin Ce's Oeuvres." *Journal of African Literature and Culture/JALC,* No. 3. IRCALC, 2006. 11-29.

Hamilton, G. A. R. "Beyond Subjectificatory Structures: Chin Ce 'In the season of another life'" *Journal of New Poetry* (v3), IRCALC 2006. 95-117.

Laye, Camara. *The Dark Child*. Trans. James Kirkup & Ernest Jones. New York: The Noonday Press, 1994.

Lévinas, Emmanuel. *Time and the Other.* Trans. Richard A. Choen. Pittsburgh, PA: Duquesne UP, 1987.

_ _ _. *Totality and Infinity: An Essay on Exteriority*. Trans. Alphonso Lingis. Pittsburgh, PA.: Duquesne UP, 1969.

Lispector, Clarice. *A hora da estrela*. Rio de Janeiro: Rocco, 1999.

_ _ _. *Água Viva*. Rio de Janeiro: Rocco, 1998.

Marques, Irene. "Mia Couto and the Holistic Choric Self: Recreating the Broken Cosmic Order (Or: Relearning the Song that Truly Speaks…)." *Journal of African Literature and Culture/JALC,* No. 4, IRCALC 2007. 101-124.

Morrison, Toni. *Beloved.* New York: Penguin Books, 2000.

Ngũgĩ, wa Thiong'o. *Decolonizing the Mind: The Politics of Language in African Literature.* London: Currey, 1986.

Okuyade, Ogaga. "Locating the Voice: The Modernist Maze of Chin Ce's *The Visitor.*" *Critical Supplement: The Works of Chin Ce*. IRCALC, 2007.135-158.

Oyono, Ferdinand. *The Old Man and The Medal.* Trans. John Reed. London: Heinemann, 1967.

Pollard, Velma. *Dread Talk: The Language of Rastafari.* Kingston, Jamaica: Canoe P, 1994.

Smith, Charles. "For God and Country: Chin Ce's *Millennial* Verses." *Critical Supplement: The Works of Chin Ce*. IRCALC, 2007. 197-205.

Suzuki, Daisetz Teitaro. *The Essentials of Zen Buddhism: Selected from the Writings of Daisetz T. Suzuki.* Ed. and Intro. Bernard Phillips. Westport, Conn.: Greenwood Press, 1973.

Théoret, France. *Entre raison et déraison: essais.* Montréal: Herbes rouges, 1987.

Toko, M. Djockoua. "Child Education in Camara Laye's *The Dark Child* and Chin Ce's *Children of Koloko.*" *Critical Supplement: The Works of Chin Ce.* IRCALC, 2007. 39-62.

Usongo, Kenneth. "Pedagogy of Disillusionment: The Case of Ferdinand Oyono's *The Old Man and the Medal* and Chin Ce's *Gamji College.*" *Critical Supplement: The Works of Chin Ce.* IRCALC, 2007. 111-134.

Whorf, Benjamin. *Language, Thought, and Reality: Selected Writings.* Cambridge: M.I.T. P, 1964.

Wordsworth, William. "Preface." *Wordsworth and Coleridge: Lyrical Ballads.* Eds. R.L. Brett and A.R. Jones. Cambridge: UP, 1963. 241-272.

2

Memory, Transition and Dialogue

THE CYCLIC ORDER OF CHIN CE'S OEUVRES

Amanda Grants

*B*eginning with *African Eclipse* Chin Ce's oeuvres foreshadow a general communal retardation most poignant in the Koloko and Gamji fictions. Seen together as one movement, Chin Ce's writings trace a movement in the major characters from one of social preoccupation to that of psychological transition in awareness and growth. 'A Farewell' highlights this movement in a prefatory manner. The three ways: left, right and middle signify three choices involving two extremes and a middle course, an important element in Chin Ce's oeuvres. Before the choice is made, we must face ourselves, our fears, and actions represented in 'only our own graffiti.' The choice of a middle alternative is imperative from the flagellation of the other extremities but it is a lonely route that marks a separation from friends, old values, and life ways. In *Children of Koloko*, Yoyo represents this third factor and his separation from his two friends, Dickie and Buff, finally marks his attainment of growth as we shall see later.

With the choice enacted in full awareness of the sense of alienation engendered, progress is sure even if the social outcome of this progress in political and social discourse may be uncertain. 'May 29 1999', a historical poem on the inauguration of Nigeria's last democracy confronts us with the grotesque physical paunch and slovenliness of Nigeria's new civilian leadership which combine with poetic epithets to forecast political disaster. 'The curse of the triangle' is another slavery which the new government portends for the generality of the Nigerian people. Ce's cynicism has been justified in the society-evident lack of direction that rated that country one of the most corrupt nations on earth under the government of a retired general Olusegun Obasanjo. It is the fraud of nation building which Africa's postcolonial founding fathers had mistaken for patriotism. Its impact on the younger generations to come is being witnessed in contemporary politics of attrition and dislocation of previously honoured traditional values, a situation that Chin Ce forewarns in his second fiction Gamji College.

'Second Cousin' continues the dialogue of the younger generation which crystallise in Chin Ce's prose fiction *Children of Koloko*. The Nigerian youth such as 'Hugo, the burly head of the thuggery squad' (Koloko 79) has metamorphosed in his 'gold and bangle epaulettes' as the 'success' story of Nigeria's upper social class even with odd jobs to his credit. His sponsors are men who, with the combination of politically motivated murders, extortion, bribery, and corruption have become governors of states or chairs of local municipal councils. Nigeria is consequently in deep political, social, and economic trouble with such fraudulence among the high and low.

'Wind and Storm' furthers the dialogue on the trouble with Nigeria from Achebe's published position on a similar subject. In this discourse, the poet avers that self-inflicted wounds are no machination of destiny, especially for a prayerful community which Nigeria has grown into with its deepening Muslim-Christian divide. The consequences of this political malady ('stoked by touts at

Government House(s)') are myriad. Environmental degradation ('craters of the Niger') is a corollary of government neglect and paucity of imaginative thinking. ('There are no more sages on silent feet.') Where the instance of leadership exists, there abounds an overstock of quasi-scholarship and religious zealotry.

'The Preacher' satirises a religious environment of pew sanctimony and its failing impact on the sensitivity of the young ones. The timeworn and consequently unimaginative religious dialogue 'let him hear who has ears' begs effective communication with frenzied gestures ('in the crescendo of agitation'). Since the sermon degenerates to boredom and 'consecrated tedium,' imagination must be given free vent in escape from the stifling environment of religious extravaganzas.

Chin Ce's delineated 'eclipse' is therefore of a postcolonial transition that can only be determined by the quality of both leadership and citizenship in contemporary African republics. The evidence of internal social contradictions and ungainly stirring in the form of political upheavals within the continent naturally justifies the cynicism with which a poet and writer like Chin Ce would draw us to the centre of the African pedagogy.

SONG, DRAMA, AND MEMORY IN *CHILDREN OF KOLOKO*

Children of Koloko marks out at initial reading as something of a childhood story of innocence. But it really isn't. What we have are character types seen through the central character, Yoyo, and other bohemian adjuncts of the central personage mainly Dickie and Buff. So we have three youngsters who are negotiating their passage into adulthood and are keenly aware of the deficiencies of their environment – and of themselves. These are therefore some kind of social critics but not in an aloof, self-righteous manner.

They are all participants in a drama of social transition and

35

psychological awareness. The result is a kind of growth. But while the society records painful imperviousness to change, the pace of psychological growth of the hero predictably outmatches all of his contemporaries. Yoyo is a kind of interrogator engaged in dialogue with society. The first part of the story introduces him as a precocious child prodigy. His imagination is definitely and highly spectroscopic.

> Heaven's clouds rolled in a beautiful surging mass of flaming blue tongues.
>
> …
>
> The clouds seemed to surge with greater momentum. Something must be happening too in the ethers, I believed. Each darting tongue of cloud was a bubble of energy flowing in space. I saw them as warriors charging on to battle against Lucifer and his own queer band of angels. I could see how they adorned themselves in grotesque sizes and shapes that kept changing and twisting and bending, now parting, then coming together to become coupled like Siamese cats. I watched calmly as they disappeared behind the veil into the unknown where the band of good angels must be standing on guard. What further threat assailed them by devil's advocates plotting to overthrow heaven and rule? (COK 17)

Coming home was, for him, an exile of a hopefully temporary nature.

> The journey was not my idea of a picnic, right from when Mam, Bap and Dora began to make preparations for our departure till we all bundled our bulks into the loaded vehicle. Not that I do not like changes as Bap did, for isn't all life full of change, as he would say. For me Boko was the only memorable event like any other place where one had grown up and got used to. So Boko had been home, if home was the house you lived and the community you had grown in, attending school each morning and picking up your habits for

over fifteen years until suddenly they said a new state was born and we had become strangers there. (24)

But he adjusts quickly to his new environment thanks to two friends he had quickly taken to and who provide him with fillers in his awareness and understanding of his new environment.

> 'I am Dickie.'
>
> 'And this is Buff,' they introduced in the manner of another dress rehearsal.
>
> 'People used to think we are twins,' Dickie said, 'and this loafer, Buff, is always flattered,' he teased.
>
> They must be such fine clowns, I concluded.
>
> Dickie was a gaunt fellow with high cheekbones and wan smile that disguised his good sense of drama. But Buff was a podgy guy who would never look strict or serious with anything even from a distance.
>
> 'Let's go and spend some time at De Mica's palm wine bar at the town square,' Buff proffered. 'I'll pay.' (29-30)

Through Dickie and Buff Yoyo learns a great deal about the backwardness and homelessness situation of this African neighbourhood called Koloko.

> 'Do you really believe that Dogkiller has seventeen wives and, over thirty-five sons and daughters' I asked Buff who only gave me a mysterious snort without an answer.
>
> 'Dickie, could this be true?' I protested. 'I mean how does he manage them?'
>
> Dickie loudly snorted too and whispered, 'How can I tell? I've never been near his New Heaven mansion.'
>
> 'I have,' quipped Buff. 'Such lavish edifice. ...Greater than any one ten

of the chiefs' put together. And as large as heaven too,' he added, 'if you have been to heaven?' he asked. (21)

Yoyo dilates quite understandably between outright rejection of the generation of his fathers and leaders such as Dogomutun and Fathead and the vicarious enjoyment of the spoils of national plunder seen in his participation in Fathead's 'house warming' ceremony. Later in 'Koloko News' we see him defending the public ridicule of his society which the likes of chief Dogkiller, the politician, had visited on it by his misappropriations of public resources.

The quality of a dramatic short fiction in *Children of Koloko* comes with its spontaneity of progression via the impetus of discourse – a salient, unique quality in the writings of Chin Ce as in 'The Bottle' (*Gamji College*). This interaction of dialogue and songs serves to convey deep social entrenchments such as the public song at chief Fathead's house warming ceremony:

When we eat, when we drink
Food, wine in steady flow
Do not guess O do not wonder
It's better life for rural hunger. (129)

Fathead's speech at this celebration reflects the confidence tricks of the privileged elite class and the false logic of those who admire them and aspire to similar material accomplishments without the basic corollary of intellectual discernment.

'Koloko mma mma o! I salute you all. Our elders say that gbata gbata is a language that has two faces. It might mean good, it might mean disaster' (98).

In this drama of social and communal acquiescence, tradition is made culprit, a situation heightened by Fathead's use of local wisdom in two proverbs, one being that 'gbata gbata is a language that has two faces; it might mean good, it might mean disaster' and the other asserting rather hypocritically: 'it is from the home front that all training must take off...' with the English equivalent of 'charity begins at home.' Of course these are mere rigmarole. The women folk who applaud him are unlike their modern enlightened liberated folks who acquiesce to the impoverishment of their nation state so long as it carves for them a niche of the social table. We may later see some rising assertions in the younger generation represented by Tina and her mother, but only briefly.

The Koloko women of Fathead's generation, through their songs and dances, are active connivers in a degenerating social order. Their songs betray the subversion of art for mere toadying in personal indulgence. To support Fathead's self-dominant dialogue, the women improvise a song from an Anglican hymn. We are shown an admixture of spiritual irreverence from poor syncretism of traditional and Christian religious worship:

The millionaire cometh!
See the millionaire cometh!
All eyes have seen him and
They say the millionaire cometh!!!(133)

Both cases, particularly the latter, are inversions of their intended meaning. With communal epithets and witticism, Fathead justifies extravagant lifestyles and social ceremony – actions that are the bane of real progress. The society applauds in another intent, as long as they are participants of the crumbs of the table. In their haste to satisfy their palate, even custom can be thrown overboard: 'A hungry man

39

does not waste the time on proverbs when the real meal is before him' (133). In the social dramatic, cheap and vulgar wit interact freely.

> 'Hey be careful how you cut the meat... like you don't have any bone in your wrist. See...see that one.'
> ...
> 'Whose name does he bear?' someone followed.
> 'Don't you mind these young boys of the end age.'
> 'No manhood in between, and no bones.'
> 'It's too much mischief with the girls.'
> 'Ha! Ha! Ha! (134)

Koloko stinks for sure. The degeneracy of any society is complete when it never questions but accepts all that is thrown at it in its craving for indulgence, much like contemporary American culture. And this is the dramatic thrust of Chin Ce's narrative: the bane of the children of Koloko (read Nigeria).

Transition and Dialogue in *Gamji College*

Gamji College (GC) begins on a staccato rhythm (GC 2) showcasing the dubious morality of the religions imported into Africa and embraced by an overwhelmed, uninformed and ignorant multitude. The story begins with a freshman's experience on his first day at school. Tai on arrival is beset by a proselyte band whose interest in his welfare is mere pretension. It strikes the new comer that the new friends foisting themselves on him are like the local politicians represented by president Baba Sonja who do not keep their words.

> James was not quite true to his words, Tai noted with a sense of disrelish. He had come at just half past six while the arrangement was for seven. Tai was just preparing to go for dinner with another

roommate called Pablo. Pablo had just checked in a few minutes ago. He was in his second year and they were just beginning to make friends. To James Tai said, 'Oh you're here,' and he tried to avoid a grimace, managing a wan smile instead.

'Yes, I can see you are ready.'

Whoever said he was ready? Tai hadn't said anything to that effect... (11)

The final dismissal of these unwanted elements is also the rejection of the politics of impoverishment and deceit represented in the persons of college rector Dr. Jeze and his uncle the 'born-again' president Baba Sonja. More importantly the imported religion is equally thrown aboard.

"You must experience God!" James warned, his desperation sounded like a drowning man's last momentous effort to hold on to a straw.

"And who is to give me the experience?" Tai snorted with derision, "Brother Rimi?" he laughed mirthlessly.

"Or Leader Obu? Oh, what of President Sonja and his ugly paunch? Now gentlemen, James and Rock-of-Peter or is it Peter-the-Rock? Please leave me. You are really being a nuisance interrupting my sleep," he pointed gently to the door.(34)

In 'The Bottle' the second part of Gamji College fiction, we are not deceived by the rowdy boisterous company that Dogo, Femi and Milord (which in Koloko may also read Yoyo, Dickie and Buff). Chin Ce's tripartite characters are metonymical of the tripod on which the Nigerian nation is said to rest, representing the tree major ethnicities that had dominated the country's political scene since independence to no apparent benefit. However, the three part characters here also present Chin Ce's three way resolution of the past present and future more clearly illustrated in *The Visitor*, his third work of fiction. The entire racy banters suggest the juvenile delinquency of the Nigerian youth on the surface. Underneath there are currents of restiveness seen later in today's threat to Nigeria's corporate existence by youths of the Niger Delta. Chin Ce clearly foresees this restiveness in the queries and exchanges of Dogo, Milord and Femi.

> 'Until you are carried back in a stretcher,' Milord retorted.
>
> 'Of course, what better VIP treatment? And I won't miss the sirens. No governor in this country ever rides the streets of the town without sirens.'
>
> 'I can get you one,' Dogo offered, 'the noisiest siren the bloodiest dictator never had.'
>
> 'Great then that's the making of a president. One secret pals, those guys are drunk or doped all the time. That's their courage to face the crowd…with all those lies.'
>
> 'And to sneak out at night to see their girlfriends…'
>
> 'And their harem,' Milord peered at Dogo.
>
> 'Talk about harem.' (55)

The youths of Gamji seem to have lost faith in the leadership which offers nothing but self aggrandisement and self indulgence. Similarly the youths, lacking a credible model, offer no reliable alternative as events following the campus elections clearly testify. Napoleon, late entrant for Gamji college union presidency, is part of the thuggery and rigging that characterise elections in Nigeria. Napoleon proposes an incredibly reactionary political alternative:

> 'You take one step back to make two steps forward. Being a neutral for once is like that, but in this case, I manipulate it to divert the votes to me. I win, and it is victory for the revolution. Actually my comrade Yusuf derailed when he allowed his tribesmen to hijack

his manifesto and that's when I decided to come in… Just come and see me deliver my manifesto,' he boasted.

'And if you fail?'

'Never,' Napoleon spat. 'No politician ever contemplates failure in this business. I'm already the chief executive of Gamji union government, and if all fails,' he made one deft movement of his right hand behind his back and fished out a pistol. 'This doesn't.' (82)

Napoleon's reliance on his gun as a last alternative to fetch him victory is as misguided as the morality of successive national elections in Africa which is simply to rule by any means necessary and, possibly, die in office. It comes as no surprise that the union elections like all Nigerian elections end in chaos and violence. The only real candidate whose manifesto appears to make sense is killed presumably by Napoleons' gun.

RETURN OF THE PRODIGAL IN *CHILDREN OF KOLOKO*

Again we must return to the book *Children of Koloko* to complete the metamorphosis of individual consciousness in a transitional society. In 'Return to Koloko,' Yoyo confesses earnestly,

> 'Six years and I was now a man. My CV was quite impressive. I had finished college, did a stint of press work, joined defence academy, and deserted. In a few months I hoped to find my professional bearing though I knew not what at present…'(COK 121)

Here dream, dialogue, and song are employed to depict changing attitudes in the consciousness of the young hero. In six years of transition Yoyo had run his wit's end at various jobs – including fatherhood – and here he is a reluctant returnee. Earlier determined on a course of total self-exile, he had never wanted to set foot on his home town any more but the strong pull to be present at grand dad's funeral reveals a quality of loyalty and citizenship in the young hero. Yoyo's dream entries had presaged the passage of the old grand parents signifying a passage of a generation. Dream recording is significant of a rising awareness of himself and the dialogue in this section is no longer lengthy for young Yoyo had other thoughts to occupy him.

> Ham drove roughly and jerkily. 'I am just coming from your compound, your old Bap's wake keeping is tonight,' he told me sanguinely.
>
> 'Is that so?' I now knew where he had had his drink.
>
> 'Oh, you didn't know this?' he remarked, and seemed a little surprised at my ignorance. I explained.' I got Mam's letter and guessed so.'
>
> 'That's tomorrow. Tonight is the keeping awake for all night,' and he proceeded to chatter through the rest of the journey but my attention was somewhere else. (COK 134)

Goodman has also changed. He now wears 'a distant contemplative expression on his face' in fulfilment of Old Bap's injunction to go into 'studied contemplation' for the rest of his life. Bap shows 'a tacit note of comprehension' towards Yoyo. The circumstance of the changing awareness may be old Bap's transition. Yoyo was not present at the funeral of Kata and Big Mam. Thus Old Bap's which he witnesses is rendered in poetic sympathy: 'Thus draped in this still silent depth of profundity, my grand dad slept (135)'.

The songs of the preceding events have paled in comparison with the funeral songs; they now carry a sombre reverence as against the comic irreverence of the earlier ones, probably due to the occasion of death.

But unlike the biblical prodigal son, Yoyo's return is not permanent. Yoyo is leaving town the next day after the burial. The suggestion of continuity is made poignant in the dialogue with the old breed who angle for a second burial suggesting attachment to the old values and ways of life. Yoyo tells Mabelle: 'The burial is over now, …I mean Old Bap is buried, and that's more important' (146) than a merely ceremonial and economically wasteful 'second' burial. Also Yoyo is thinking he should be getting back to (his) own life and more especially back to (his) child and her mother….(146). Here a new attitude of introspective cognition (thought/memory) rather than the interactive sessions (dialogue) emerges from the discourse of the old breed and two young members of the new generation, being Yoyo and Dora. Dora avoids everyone's eyes with 'placid disinterest.' The narrator remarks that her capacity to retain her opinions to herself, which surpassed that of the Virgin Mary, had given him a clue as to the new attitude of goodwill he must show his people. It is not the critical, deprecatory attitude of past story narratives. It is the goodwill from a mutual parting of ways made smooth by the deeper level of understanding that had been foreshadowed in *An African Eclipse*:

> I have chosen now the day is bright
> (the shining light of
> soul lights) the middle lonely route. (3)

For young Yoyo it is a lonely route to an era devoted an understanding an acceptance of an onus of self-responsibility.

TIME, MEMORY AND ILLUSION IN *THE VISITOR*
The Visitor, described as actually Chin Ce's first work of fiction but third in his published series, takes an entirely new approach to modern story telling in Africa. It is a story in which three dimensions

of existence affecting three principal players Erie, Mensa, and Deego interrelate continuously to create an unbreakable thread and posit a statement on the continuation of individual responsibility over and above mere existential needs. The philosophy behind the whole story seems to be predicated upon an Igbo traditional song a translation of the main part which appears before the story:

> We are visitors upon this earth
> This world is not our own
> We have come but to a market place
> Only to purchase and go home

It would be therefore correct to state that the story teller is here concerned with the individual's quest for wholeness (the search for purpose) signified in Erie's lost memory (TV 1). For the hero, the discovery of who he is, and what he was, spans three paradigms of awareness –the past, present and future earlier mentioned. Erie, Mensa, and Deego are therefore same individuals as are Zeta, Sena, and Sarah in Chin Ce's deliberate tripartite also signified in the three suns of Erin ancestral land.

The setting in the future (2040) comes to us in the end part of the story as an epilogue and we are surprised to realise the whole story may have been cut from a movie which the viewer Deego had watched the night before he dozes off into an entirely strange adventure of a past dimension of reality. The movie scenes apparently trigger some series of experiences which draw back to a past history of crime and death featuring Mensa in 1994. In this Nigerian city called Aja, a cult mentality permeates the society and the youths have lost their sense of values. Yet this past is integrated within another world (Erin land) of an advanced line of kinsmen who live up to their roles as healers and teachers of the race. Mensa now called Erie in the land of his ancestors must go back and retrieve his memory lost from the gun blast that took his life on earth, the story goes.

Mensa is the product of the herd syndrome and violence that riddle the nation and threaten to destroy its entire fabric of existence. Unlike Yoyo, he never graduates from college. His drop out of school is the natural consequence of his denial of creative and positive existence, and added with his misguided involvement in the quest of revenge, Mensa's destruction appears a foregone conclusion. The 1994 story of Mensa is seen partly through his narrative consciousness and through the omniscient narrative point of view to embrace a world of police corruption and decadence in Nigeria, a country drowning in its own degenerate materialism. All it offers may just be frustration and disappointment at all levels, a frustration that permeates Mensa's efforts and dogs all his noxious attempts at identity through cult power.

> Ironi alone of all the others enjoyed tacit state patronage and confidence. It warmed his heart to know then that the minister of petroleum was one of the financiers of the club. Thus even as a job seeker Ironi connection guaranteed a niche among the notables of the society in which he had sought social acceptance, if only he could work hard enough in service to earn his cut and launch himself into wealth and power!
>
> How could it have been otherwise? Better put, why did it become otherwise now? (TV 40)

In contrast to this world is Erin, the land of the ancestors as a present reality. Chin Ce's entry into the subjective universe of ancestral interactivity offers a unique perspective on contemporaneous and simultaneous levels of existence. Surprisingly in this world of the ancestors is a highly advanced city, where even the memory of the individual members of the race can be retrieved and

47

preserved for healing purposes or for posterity. The ancestral universe is thus not unlike the parallel worlds of modern science fiction where the author must have drawn his influence. But the idyllic representation of this world of ancestors as custodian of the African heritage is a product of a conscious artiste who wishes to consolidate the belief in the potential of a race through the emergence of a progeny who will eventually take charge of the transcendent qualities of heritage. Thus Mensa now as Erin is seen living another existence in Erin City – a temporary existence that offers recovery from the modernist adventurism of his physical life.

> It plagued him daily to walk about the walls of the city like some disembodied entity, a ghost whose only memory of his identity comes in flashes and hunches.
> 'You are at home among your spirits,' Zeta's granddad told him. 'But you will not understand, and it were better you did not ask too much questions. Take those daydreams, visions and nightmares as natural as the colour of your tan, things which will continue to hold little value to you until you come to face your past in order to know the moment. (22)

This spiritual universe which comes in grasps or strains of recollection and where time and values are of a different scale is quite unlike that of the terrestrial plane. Thus the process of healing may take some time not only for Erie but for the whole society afflicted by the plague of displacement and lack of sympathy.

> The city of his fathers looked all strange to him. Broad cleanly swept roads and walkways. All so real too. But then reality he had now learnt was a relative thing. He couldn't believe he had lived here for seven years, seven good years that seemed like seven hundred years in earth's span and still no concrete or tangible

evidence of who he truly was. (22)

Finally the time comes, almost too soon, for Erie to withdraw from this idealised world of communal empathy to face the full details of his actions as Mensa on the physical terrain. The rest of the story moves quickly leading to the summation of characters in the story and their relationship with one another. Important characters in this part include Sena and Omo, both allies of Mensa in the robbery and search for vengeance. The deaths of the characters come in swift ironic successions both allies dying by the hand of their friend Mensa, and Mensa finally falling to summary execution by armed militia men by which the Nigerian society, where the setting is derived, is sorely notorious for. In the replay of the death experience, Mensa's memory is transferred to Erie who now metamorphoses in Erin City with a wider perspective of his part in the rhythm of life. Erie discovers that Zeta (Sena) has been there all the time and both of them must continue the quest for further understanding of themselves and their lives' purpose.

The Visitor is a blend of the subjective consciousness in a serious quest for identity. True to opinion (TV1), it will remain a serious challenge to the traditional view of time and reality as a linear or progressive sequence of events. This is an important attribute of Chin Ce's oeuvres. His approach to fiction in Africa may appear to hold some significance beyond the ordinary and subjective perspective of social reality. In comparison to Lawrence's idea of art as assisting in the living of life to the fullest (Sons xvii), Ce's cyclic universe of memory, transition and dialogue undoubtedly presents a deeper conception of art, and of life, that centres on the individual's perception of his unique position in society.

NOTES

[1]In its introduction, it is stated that Gamji College 'is the same tragedy of misplaced values, directionlessness and exhibition of political charisma bred on the stable of ethnic chauvinism that we have seen in *Children of Koloko.*'

[2] In The Trouble with Nigeria Chinua Achebe states mater-of-factly that 'the trouble with Nigeria is simply and squarely' a failure of leadership, a point which Chin Ce corroborates in entirety in "Bards and Tyrants" (ALJ B5 2005).

WORKS CITED

Ce, Chin. *An African Eclipse and other poems*. Enugu: Handel Books 2000.

–––. *Children of Koloko*. Enugu: Handel Books 2001.

–––. *The Visitor*. Lagos: Handel Books 2005.

–––. *Gamji College*. Enugu: Handel Books 2002.

Delores, Vine Jnr. *God Is Red: A Native View of Religion*. Colorado: Fulcrum Publishing, 1994.

Lawrence, D. H. *Sons and Lovers*. London: Penguin Books, 1963.

The Short and Longer Fictions

3

Educating the Child

LAYE'S *THE DARK CHILD* AND CE'S *CHILDREN OF KOLOKO*
Djockoua Manyaka Toko

INTRODUCTION

*T*his study gives an insight into child education in multicultural
societies. It specifically targets African societies where western
civilization more and more encroaches on African traditions.
Examining two bildungsromane: Camara Laye's The *Dark Child*
(DC)[1] and Chin Ce's *Children of Koloko* (COK), respectively set in
the Guinean and Nigerian societies, this paper argues that despite
some points of divergence, both texts present African traditional
values as the foundation stone of child education. These traditions,
though some may be discarded, are a springboard to the African
child's mastery of western technology and science. In Laye's novel,
the tension between the traditional caste system, the Koranic and
French schools is resolved by the parents' and the community's deep
reverence for these cultural values. In Ce's novel, although the
capitalist unbridled craze for money and power has perverted
postcolonial Koloko, Yoyo attains growth due to his attachment to
African wisdom and cultural values that he successfully blends with
western science and technology. In the two works, the main

protagonists thus opt for what Amanda Grants calls "a middle course."[2]

WESTERN COLONISATION AND THE AFRICAN WRITER'S RESPONSE

Colonization, leading to the hybridization of African societies has generated heated debates on the type of education that should be imparted to the African child. In his article "Hegel on Education," Allen W. Wood notes that education, "has to do with the activities of school, their pupils, teachers or tutors (including parents) and their students, whether they are children or adolescents" (20). Wood's analysis that examines the various meanings of the Hegelian "Bildung" focuses on the key components of education: the learning of specific skills, the imparting of knowledge, good judgment and wisdom, as well as the imparting of culture from generation to generation. Education is thus a tripartite process that involves the environment (natural and social environments), the trainer (educator) and the child (the trainee).

This truism carries great weight today in most African societies where African traditions are more than ever before, jeopardized by globalization and the challenges of western culture. This phenomenon thus raises many questions: What is the responsibility of African parents and societies in child education? What type of education should be imparted to the African child today in a twenty-first century world marked by a flood of mass media and hi-tech that tends to standardize cultures? In *Homecoming*, Ngugi wa Thiong'o holds that:

> The real snake was surely monopoly capitalism, whose very condition of growth is cut-throat competition, inequality and oppression of one group by another. It was capitalism and its external manifestations, imperialism, colonialism, neo-colonialism, that had disfigured the African past. (45)

Continuing the argument, Ngugi further professes:

> ... in order that one group, one race, one class (and mostly a minority) can exploit another group, race or class (mostly the majority), it must not only steal its body, batter and barter it for thirty pieces of silver, but must steal its mind and soul as well...Through the school system, he can soothe the fears of the colonized, or make them at least connive at the rationale behind capitalist exploitation. (45)

If monopoly capitalism disfigured the African past, generated egocentrism and an exacerbated quest for wealth, today, this quest overrules the key precept of communal good that underpins education in traditional African communities. Kashim Ibrahim Tala points out that "pre-capitalist African society subsists on the social philosophy of the greatest good of the greatest number. In other words, collective responsibility is the very essence of ancestral authority" (Epasa Moto 158). Incorporating this precept, the ideological matrix that prevailed in pre-colonial Africa guaranteed a symbiosis between the individual and the group. Consequently, from this golden rule, derived a whole pedagogy, which, using African folklore, taught the child sound values such as communal good, compassion, mutual aid, truthfulness, the sense of right and wrong, spontaneity, and love of man and nature. Before the Negritude movement, this ideological matrix was celebrated in *Adventures of Huckleberry Finn*, Mark Twain's nineteenth-century masterpiece where Huck Finn, the white teenager, wholeheartedly espouses Jim's (the African slave's) ideology rooted in the above-cited values. Thus, earlier than Chinua Achebe's *Things Fall Apart*, and Camara Laye's *The Dark Child, Adventures of Huckleberry Finn* was already in the nineteenth century, a strong advocate of African cultural values.

In African literature, the celebration of he untainted African traditions reverberates in the bildungsroman or the coming of age story. Jerome Buckley, explaining the German origin of the bildungsromane in *Seasons of Youth*, argues that while "roman" means novel, "bildung" connotes "portrait," "picture," "shaping," and "formation," which all converge to the idea of development or creation. "The development of the child can also be seen as the creation of the man" (13-14). The bildungsromane thus revolves around childhood, a recurrent theme in African literature. Maxwell Okolie posits that "childhood, like the past with which it is associated, occupies a prominent psychological part of African literature." In his words,

> the evocation of individual childhood, calls up as a corollary the evocation of Africa's 'childhood' itself, which, in effect, is an indirect apology and illustration of its splendour before the advent of colonization. ... Rediscovering this glory is in a way an indirect exhortation to the Africans engrossed in the pursuit of Westernization and its allurements, to retrace their steps back to the honourable values they are inclined to despise thus re-equipping themselves with the pride of their worth and the psychological reassurance vital to their existence and rejuvenation. (35)

Like Ngugi, Okolie points an accusing finger at western culture and its impingement on African traditions. Both Ngugi's and Okolie's statements will lay the foundations of this analysis which seeks to prove that despite the prevalent cult of Westernization in modern African societies, African genuine and positive cultural values are the stepping stone of a successful African child education.

The Dark Child and *Children of Koloko* are possibly two bildungsromane that retrace the lives of two protagonists from childhood to maturity. Far from being mere evocations of childhood experiences, both works pose the crucial problem of the African child's growth in the contemporary global village. They bring to the limelight the encroachments of western civilization on African traditions and their impact on the African trainee. Comparing the two, this study shows analogies and differences in the protagonists, their training and growth. It focuses on the three main factors of child education: the society (the settings of the novels), the training (the way education is imparted) and the trainee (the impact of education on the protagonists and their subsequent response and growth).

TRADITIONAL EDUCATION IN *THE DARK CHILD*
The Dark Child, an autobiographical novel, furthers the Negritude aim to uphold African values that were jettisoned under slavery and colonization. The novel outlines the conflict between African traditions and Western culture imposed by colonization. Though Camara Laye from his country of exile (he was writing from France) revives the memory of the mythological Africa, he overtly presents himself as the prototype of the modern African who hovers between the black tradition and the white civilization. In contrast to Deicy Jiménez who argues that Laye's work "shows the African struggle and search for an identity in colonial times" (CASA), this paper asserts that the struggle and search for identity in the work is a contemporary quest in postcolonial African societies.

Laye's autobiographical novel is divided into three main sections that show the protagonist's development from childhood to maturity. The first section that may be titled "Childhood," covers the first five chapters (1-5). This part of the book depicts the family's compound at Kouroussa where the child comes into contact with the family totem. The totem is a small black snake, the guiding spirit of the family. As the father enlightens the boy on the small snake, the clash between traditional education and the colonial school already looms: "I fear, I very much fear, little one, that you are not often enough in my company. You are all day at school, and one day you will depart from that school for a greater one. You will leave me, little one…" (27). This statement uncovers the parent's fear: the father, a famous goldsmith knows that he will pass to his elder son neither the totemic tradition, nor the profession of his caste. Even at Tindican (the mother's village) where the child spends his holiday among a loving grandmother and innumerable kind playmates, the young boy does not really feel part of the village community. He will not therefore inherit his mother's magic power and her crocodile totem despite his rite of passage that is carried on in the second section. The second section of the autobiography "Years of Initiation" (chapters 6-8), recalls the boy's experiences both in the Koranic and the French schools which are the first steps of the protagonist's initiation.

The trek to the sacred place (a prelude to circumcision), the enormous baobab tree at the junction of the Komoni River, and the mysterious Konden Diara stratagem instill fear and at the same time teach the Guinean young men to overcome their fright. The protagonist's initiation is then achieved through a long journey in the forest. However, even at the apex of this initiation rite, the reader perceives the narrator's fear that one day, the white culture will annihilate this traditional practice that gives rise to a village feast, to a community communion. During the dancing ceremony, the new men are presented objects, symbols of their allegiance to their fathers' castes (professions). Unlike other boys who are shown articles that are related to their fathers' professions, the protagonist is shown an exercise-book and a fountain pen, embodiments of the white culture. Here, once more, the boy is gradually taken away from his tradition. He is on his way to exile which the final section of the book concretizes. The last part of the text "Exile" (chapters 9-12), depicts two different types of departure: the journey to Conakry after the narrator has been admitted into the technical high school and the longer journey to France where he will learn engineering.

In this bildungsroman, the family is the bedrock of the boy's education. The young boy's "relationship with his parents is the link between the child and his African roots" (CASA). Both the mother and the father assume responsibility by monitoring the son's education. They see to it that the boy imbibes the fundamental values of African culture: the sense of community and solidarity that characterize social relations in African communities. John Mbiti holds that in the traditional African community, an individual only exists as an element of a group. Joining Mbiti, Kange Ewane, a Cameroonian historian, argues that in the African context, animate and inanimate beings commune in the same unit of life and participation. Within such a context, solidarity is not assistance with a taint of condescension: it is rather a vital necessity; it becomes co-possession and co-utilization (*Semence et moisson* 62). The protagonist's father thus teaches the son this principle by example. He is himself a good model to the youth: "I have nothing which other men have not also, and even that I have less than others, since I give everything away, and would even give away the last thing I had, the shirt on my back" (*DC* 25). The father has been given the totem, the guiding spirit because he is "the most worthy" member of his tribe (25). Being "the most worthy" implies possessing and respecting everlasting values such as the sense of solidarity, compassion, spontaneity, and the precept of communal good inherent in African culture.

The father and the mother thus teach the young boy the powers of the natural world. They introduce him to the small snake, the totem of the family which embeds customs, beliefs, morals and discipline handed over from one generation to the other. In fact in the novel, the family and the society at large are conducive to child education. The father instructs his son: "Take care never to deceive anyone. ... Be upright in thought and deed. And God will be with you" (182). The hero's education is successfully carried out thanks to three elements that Laye regards as key actors in the education of a child: a stable family (parents), the school, and a viable society. William Plomer notes that "where [Camara] grew up, the sense of community is implicit and inherent. Tradition and long usage have created politeness, correctness, mutual respect, and simple dignity" (*Current Concerns*). The narrator himself highlights this point in his statement: "I lived actually amidst a deeply united family where all domestic quarreling was strictly forbidden" (150). In other terms, this assertion implies that a peaceful environment is a primordial requirement for child education. When the young trainee moves to Conakry, a bigger town, Uncle Mamadou, whom the narrator describes as being "tall and strong, always very correctly dressed, calm and dignified"(150), perpetuates these values. He thus ensures the continuity in the imparting of culture from generation to generation.

After the family and the community at large have laid solid foundations of the child's moral and spiritual education, they can now hand him over to the western school that will teach him science and technology as the father rightly points out:

> Each one follows his own destiny, my son. Men cannot change what is decreed. Your uncles too have had an education...This opportunity is within your reach. You must seize it. You've already seized one, seize this one too, make sure of it. There are still so many things to be done in our land.... Yes, I want you to go to France. [....] Soon we'll be needing men like you here. (182)

Camara's father and mother understand that though the child may lose some of his traditional cultural values, his mastery of science and technology is useful to the community. Here again, the African traditional principle of "co-possession and co-utilization" underpins the father's decision. When the parent observes that "soon we'll be needing men like you here," he implicitly advises the son not to forget his allegiance and duty to his community. Although this blend may not eradicate the tension that arises from the contrast between African and western cultures, it lessens it and thus validates G. N. Marete's view that there is absence of conflict in the narrator's maturation (*Childhood* 93). In effect making a choice is the protagonist's dilemma: "And I was no longer sure whether I ought to continue to attend school or whether I ought to remain in the workshop: I felt unutterably confused" (DC 27). But the narrator's indecision is short-lived as it is quickly resolved by his father's order: "Go now" (27). Later the parent never mentions the little black snake again to the son (28). The male parent's decision portends a choice: the son must attend the western school. This choice releases the tension that reoccurs in the last chapter when the boy is faced with the mother's objection to his departure to France. At the end of the novel, the metro map given to the young traveler by the director (the school headmaster) symbolizes guidance, orientation, knowledge, and conquest. It is a tool that will enable the African child to reach Argenteuil, the new environment where he has to complete his training.

The African community thus monitors the child's education from the opening to the close of the novel, giving the action its linearity. As a result, the narrator's departure to France is not, as Jiménez mentions, "the metaphor of the social and cultural oblivion of his African roots" (CASA). It is rather a symbolic appropriation of western technology and science to the benefit of the African (Guinean) community. When the father punctuates that: "Your uncles too have had an education," he covertly refers to the "middle course" that is neither the abrogation of western culture nor "oblivion" of African roots. Uncle Mamadou, whom the boy "regarded as a saintly personage" (151), successfully imbeds both African and western cultures. By the end of the novel the reader infers that the narrator will follow the same course, thus fulfilling his promise to his male parent: "I will come back" (DC

182). The same promise is reiterated to Marie: "Surely I would be coming back" (188). "Coming back" to Guinea symbolizes a return home (to roots) with the much needed science and technology that may enhance the economic development of Guinea.

CAPITALISM AND CHILD EDUCATION IN *CHILDREN OF KOLOKO*
Unlike *The Dark Child*, Chin Ce's *Children of Koloko*, written more than three decades after Laye's book, is set in a postcolonial African country (Nigeria). Colonization has given way to neo-colonization, and monopoly capitalism has permeated most of the genuine positive African values depicted in the first novel. *Children of Koloko* thus presents the turbulent community of Koloko where communal good, compassion, mutual aid, truthfulness, the sense of right and wrong, spontaneity, and love of man and nature have been replaced by a monomaniacal pursuit for money and power. Within such a context, Ngugi's statement that "capitalism had disfigured the African past" rightly applies to Ce's novel. The craze for wealth has established corruption, thievery, drunkenness, egocentrism, and violence as commonplace practices. In the second episode, "Coming to Koloko," there is a metaphoric representation not only of postcolonial Nigeria but of most post-independence African countries ridden with disunity and turbulence:

> Koloko was not much like one had thought. The very name which sounded to me like the noise of empty gallons falling on dry earth -- ko-ko-lo-ko-- was now something else beyond my little imagination. As we drove past the Market Square, in the heart of the town, I saw that the road meandered right through as if splitting the town in two. Now who would live in a town split in halves? Koloko didn't look good at all. (27)

The town is characterized by division discernible in its various social strata and economic classes: the rich include Dogkiller,

Fathead and the numerous unscrupulous businessmen. The poor comprise teachers like Old Bap, and Bap, small workers that are involved in petty jobs, crapulous men and women who spend their time at De Mika's (JJC, Da Kata), and a group of youths whose rascality and crapulousness rival the elders'. Da Aina, head of the women, and the main female social critic in the book, clearly points at the causes of the prevalent depravity of the community: 'The elders have spoiled the village...because they lost the wisdom to teach their young who look up to them' (102). Both old and young people are corrupted by their craze for monetary gratification that undermines their morals and sense of common good. Yesterday, young people used to respect their elders, women used to respect their husbands, and the husbands used to give them their due. But today, women and young people join the elders in off licenses where all indulge in vices. Their inebriety thus reflects their irresponsibility and failure to build stable families and a stable nation. The population of Koloko is thus divided into three groups:

> Koloko had a lot of men whom you didn't get to see except in a season like Christmas. There were fat folks whose bulging eyes and beefy cheeks probably only served to frighten children. There were the returnees: young men, polished and dressed to reflect the places they lived and worked. There were those you could see were struggling to make a living and look respectable in their lavish dressing. [...]These were Koloko's children. (130)

Despite the dissimilitude that exists among the members of the various groups, each social stratum imbeds the numerous foibles and deficiencies of the society. The fat folks' "bulging eyes and beefy cheeks" signal affluence and greed. These folks overfeed on the masses' sweat and their ill-gotten wealth and authority separate them from the children they are supposed to educate. The returnees, who experience economic hardships, cover up their misery by lavish dressing, a veneer of wealth that badly conceals their struggle to make a living. As for the bad-tempered youths that harbor "mischievous grins," they have lost the childhood primeval innocence while the elders, a symbol of wisdom and dignity in traditional African societies, no longer typify these values despite their great attempts at dignity. In this perverted environment, as Grants notes:

> three youngsters ... are negotiating their passage into adulthood ... keenly aware of the deficiencies of their environment- and of themselves. [...] They are all participants in a drama of social transition and psychological awareness. The result is a kind of growth. (*JALC* 14)

Koloko contrasts sorely with Kouroussa; it is hardly an appropriate environment for child education; Buff's and Dickie's (the protagonist's friends') education is thus impaired in such a locale. These teenagers acquire neither the perennial moral and spiritual values of African culture, nor the science and technology of the western school. While Buff's failure to get admission into college causes his decision to become a businessman in the North, Dickie's three unsuccessful attempts to go to college lead him to schizophrenia. It is not only the town that is split in halves. Most of the city dwellers, though descendants of the same ancestor, do not share many things in common: "they have fallen apart" in a community where sound values are transformed into a general make-believe. The inhabitants of Koloko are split subjects in quest of an identity in a community whose traditional moral values, guideposts of pre-capitalist African societies, are uprooted.

Dogkiller's complex of superiority, his mansion, his love for lavish titles, and his avoidance of close-ups (35) mask his dwarf-size, wrinkled face and a shallow bogus identity constructed on flimsy foundations. Fathead, an exhibitionist, harangues the crowd by citing his numerous donations to curb a dire need for praise (132). His false modesty aims at rationalizing his profligacy and egocentrism manifest in his fleet of cars and mansion that have engulfed so much money in a town that lacks basic infrastructures. Fathead's 'generosity' is a semblance that does not match the African traditional principle of "co-possession and co-utilization." His 'generosity' is assistance with a taint of condescension; it sharply contrasts Camara's father's generosity in *The Dark Child*. Dickie, the schizophrenic is a split subject par excellence in Ce's novel. His schizophrenia is an outcome of economic and psychological violence that leads to frustration, drug addiction (the smoking of weed), and finally to madness, a sort of retreat from a stifling society. This retreat confers freedom on the schizophrenic as Deleuze and Guattari point out:

> Such a man [the schizo] produces himself as a free man, irresponsible, solitary and joyous, finally able to say and do something simple in his own name, without asking permission; a desire lacking nothing, a flux that overcomes barriers and codes, a name that no longer designates any ego whatever. (131)

Overcoming barriers and codes that engender repression, Dickie can openly chastise his community and party bigwigs in particular:

> All their hidden crimes in community history were revealed to Dickie in regular moments of mystic illumination and he dutifully hollered the secrets to the roof tops and street corners in the wee hours of every morning. (179)

Dickie's violence against his townsmen and bigwigs is a replica of the same violence he has been subjected to during his childhood. His invectives against Koloko's bigwigs are criticisms against a materialistic money-minded upper class that has set numerous barriers that impede the youths' economic and psychological growth.

To attain growth, Yoyo has to transcend these barriers. As Grants observes, "while the society records painful imperviousness to change, the pace of psychological growth of the hero predictably outmatches all of his contemporaries" (14). In effect, among the three friends, only Yoyo succeeds in going to college; his success and later maturity are attributable to three factors: the community's ethics at Boko where he was born and spent the early years of his childhood, his family background (Old Bap's presence at Koloko), and his departure to Gamji College. The first episode of the novel, "Last day in Boko," shows Yoyo's feelings about his natal land:

> If I had to break my silver cord with Boko, I thought, then I might as well have the rest of what's left of this morning, feel the sky, feel the ground, re-live every bit of what came to mind about the little province of Boko where I was born and grew before leaving it for good. (17)

Boko, like Kouroussa and Tindican in *The Dark Child*, is a peaceful provincial environment that favors Yoyo's communion with the natural world. He learns to understand the "mysteries" of nature that, in the Emersonian terms, "never wears a mean appearance" (Cain 479). Nature in this sense exemplifies purity, honesty, and truthfulness, values that are transmitted to Yoyo before he goes to Koloko. His relationship with the ants: "I always had a great respect for the ant community...great workaholics!" (COK19) shows his attachment to community life and communal good. He is amazed at the way ants always find their way back home, and he makes it a duty to bring back home blackhead, the wandering ant: "But as I gently picked up the blackhead with the stick and brought it near the dark hole, I knew a home was almost ready for this adventurer and his kind" (22). Providing a home to the ant is both a sign of generosity as well as a metaphor that forecasts Yoyo's later commitment to home at Koloko and to his ancestral roots despite his stay at Gamji College and his internship at the northern Trium Press. At Boko, Yoyo's father stands for authority, discipline and order: "And there stood daddy, whom all of us called Bap, a huge thundering demigod. My legs shrank at the prospect of confronting the violent rage that shook the face and hands of Bap (22). Yoyo is afraid of Bap whenever he misbehaves because Bap represents sanction and the son's bad conscience. Yet Bap can also be gentle and communicative: "Bap said with a fond and gentle pat on my head, 'C'mon son, it's time to pack your things. We are going home. We are going back to Koloko'" (22). Bap thus combines strictness, gentleness and communication, indispensable elements to child education. Before his journey to Koloko, the father's home state, Yoyo has imbibed all the African values necessary to child education. At Boko, Yoyo's playmates Nunu, Ngoo and Tukur resemble the narrator's kind playmates in *The Dark Child*. They lack Buff's and Dickie's precocity and rascality. When he arrives Koloko, Yoyo is constantly with Buff and Dickie who initiate him into drunkenness and teach him some means he can use to know and adapt to his new environment. Yet the boy is more influenced by his grandfather (Old Bap) who becomes his role model. In Koloko's society fraught with immorality, Old Bap is an icon of morality and dignity ('consequency'), while his wife (Old Mam) and her sister (Da Kata) who abuse and fight each other symbolize 'inconsequency'. When the two crones use all sorts of bad names during their quarrels, Old Bap only mutters: "'This inconsequency is becoming too much'" (52). Although he addresses the two querulous old women, Old Bap targets his society where fights are daily issues. As the chairman of the Peace Council, he has to settle innumerable conflicts:

> He seemed to have too much work in his hands for every house in Koloko had a fight, a quarrel and perhaps a curse to settle. The circle revolved viciously seven days a week and even on God's day

of rest. (53)

This turbulent setting is diametrically opposed to Tindican, Kourroussa and Uncle Mamadou's home where "all domestic quarreling was strictly forbidden." (150). As his community's peacemaker, Old Bap shows his commitment to the group. In other words, Old Bap has been chosen as Chairman of the Peace Council because, like Camara's father in *The Dark Child*, he is "the most worthy" (25). A former mission school teacher, Old Bap, Bap, his son, and later Yoyo, his grandson, blend African traditions and western education. It is this blend or 'middle course' that explains the hero's positive balance sheet at the end of his education:

> I had begun to consider myself a man of my own world. After all my CV was quite impressive I had finished college, done a stint of press work, joined national defence academy, deserted almost immediately and in the few months ahead, I hoped to find my bearing although I knew not what it would be at present. Did I add I was a father too? (167)

However, this positive balance sheet is somewhat tainted by the protagonist's short-lived jobs. This job instability poses the question of the quality and usefulness of western education dispensed in modern Nigeria and in many other postcolonial African countries since the 1990s. JJC castigates this education when he tells Buff, Dickie and Yoyo that "'You knows it's a rotten system you operate here. Your education is in shambles y' know?'" (65). This statement replicates Ce's argument in "Bards and Tyrants":

> The 1990s Nigeria witnessed the final crumbling of all that constituted its educational heritage…The social impact of degenerate education in Nigeria had taken its toll by the high incidence of unemployed graduates, the collapse of its economy and the erosion of cultural values. (ARI)

Due to its fallen standards and its unsuitability for the present job market in which cutthroat competition obtains, education for many African youths since the 1990s has given rise to bitter critique. In most African countries today, many youths and parents echo De Mika's brother's statement: "'No job anywhere for school-leavers'" (COK 66). Western education is thus open to critique not just because of the youths' awareness of rampant unemployment, but because of its problematic teaching strategies that have supplanted traditional African pedagogy.

CONCLUSION

In Camara Laye's *The Dark Child* and Ce's *Children of Koloko*, the education of the child starts by the trainee's (the child hero) mastery of the natural environment and his/her African cultural values. Camara Laye's and Ce's protagonists may have been strengthened in nature (vegetation, rivers, animals etc.) through their ritualistic journeys and exposure to folklore and tradition. However, the moral and spiritual values ingrained in African culture are more and more eroded by monopoly capitalism in Ce's *Children of Koloko*. To curtail these deleterious effect of western school and monopoly capitalism on African culture, the African child is taught positive traditions at family and community levels, the "Village meeting" in *Children of Koloko* being a good example. The cognizance of these basic principles of African communal life ensures the child's future mastery and exploitation of modern science and technology skills. In a way, Laye and Ce are saying that Westernization and globalization may threaten African traditions, but genuine traditional values will prevail if they are made the cornerstone in the education of the African child.

NOTES

[1] *The African Child* was the first translation of the original title *L'enfant noir* of Camara Laye's novel. The edition used in this work is entitled *The Dark Child*.

[2] In "Memory, Transition and Dialogue: The Cyclic Order of Chin Ce's Oeuvres," Amanda Grants notes that "the three ways: left, right and middle signify three choices involving two extremes and a middle course, an important element in Chin Ce's oeuvres (JALC 11).

WORKS CITED

Buckley, Hamilton Jerome. *Seasons of Youth. The Bildungsroman from Dickens to Golding.* Cambridge: Harvard University Press, 1974.

Ce, Chin. "Bards and Tyrants: Literature, Leadership and Citizenship Issues of Modern Nigeria." *African Literary Journal* B5 2005. 19 Dec. 2006.<http://www.africaresearch.org/Bards.htm>

– – –. *Children of Koloko.* (PDF). Enugu: Handel Books Ltd., 2001.

Courlander, Harold. *A Treasury of African Folklore.* New York: Crown Publishers Inc., 1975.

Deleuze, Gilles, Felix Guattari. *Anti-Oedipus: Capitalism and Schizophrenia.* Trans. Robert Hurley, Mark Seem and Helene R. Lane, Athlone Press, 2000.

Emerson, Ralph Waldo. *Nature. American Literature.* Vol.1. Ed. William E. Cain. New York: Pearson Education Inc., 2004. 477-515.

Ewane, Kange F. *Semence et moisson coloniales: Un regard d'africain sur l'histoire de la colonisation.* Yaounde: Editions CLE, 1985.

Grants, Amanda. "Memory, Transition and Dialogue: The Cyclic Order of Chin Ce's Oeuvres." *Journal of African Literature and Culture.* IRCALC: 2006. 11-29.

Jiménez, Deicy. Camara Laye's "The Dark Child: The undecided world of a mental mulatto." *LA CASA DE ASTERIÓN.* Vol. 5. No. 19 Barranquilla: Oct.-Nov.-Dec. 2004. 15 May 2006. http://casadeasterion.*homestead.com/v5n19dark.html*)..

Laye, Camara. *The Dark Child.* Trans. James Kirkup & Ernest

Jones. New York: The Noonday Press, 1994.

Ngugi, wa Thiong'o. *Homecoming*. London. Heinemann, 1972.

Okolie, Maxwell. "Childhood in African Literature: A Literary Perspective." *Childhood in African Literature*. Eds. Eldred Durosimi Jones & Marjorie Jones. Oxford: James Currey Ltd., 1998. 29-35.

Plomer, William. "The Dark Child: The Autobiography of an African Boy by Camara Laye." *Current Concerns* 4 (2004). 25 Oct. 2005. http://www.currentconcerns.ch/archive/2004/ 04/20040414.php

Tala, Kashim Ibrahim. "The Critical Ideological Possibilities of African Orature." *Epasa Moto*. Vol. 1 No. 2. Eds. Etienne Ze Amvela & Charles Atangana Nama. Buéa: University of Buéa Press, (Jan. 1995). 155-169.

Wood, Allen W. "Hegel on Education." *Philosophy as Education*. Ed. Amélie O. Rorty. London: Routledge, 1998. 1-28.

4

Forging One's Own?

AFRICAN AND AFRICAN-AMERICAN ENGLISH IN CE'S *CHILDREN OF KOLOKO*
AND MORRISON'S *BELOVED*

Cope, J. S.

Chester, K. A.

*I*f they brought very little with them from the old world two
centuries earlier, European immigrants certainly brought their
mother tongue and established its sovereignty in the new world. Thus
the English language belongs to white persons in ante- and post-
bellum nineteenth-century America. African-American characters
such as in Toni Morrison's *Beloved* illustrate at length how white
persons use the English language both to name and characterize
phenomena, to make sense of their world, as well as to help
perpetuate the myths of racial superiority.

Born into a civilization of white hegemony –cultural and, of
course, linguistic– the African-American, if he is cunning, will steal
the property of his master –his language– and use it against him as a
retaliatory weapon. But the novels also demonstrate that the African-
American culture is capable of creating its own language –not simply
a variation of Standard English, be it better or worse, but a language
characterized by the nature of its communication rather than by its

structure. The African-American language that Morrison presents seems to rival, in the case of characters who establish and use it, any attempts on their part to borrow and implement the tongue of their white masters. Their own language is like the antithesis of what was brought to America from England and deposited there: the language of thesis, of English. While the latter corrodes them the former is unique to their own experiences, has healing properties and, lastly, enables its speakers to communicate with mysterious and startling efficacy. It is, in brief, theirs. It is derived from English but resonates with the uniqueness of their unfortunate place in American history; it evokes their culture, the events and vignettes in which they and their ancestors were spiritually formed.

Since the African-American had little to no identity in the first place as a slave, we should not wonder that his/her language, which emerged in proportion as he/she was freed physically and spiritually, should retain the powerful marks of something that was seminal, something that was forged as men and women were forged, something that was used for the first time in situations that helped define a new race in a new world. When the English language is taken unleavened from the whites it perverts the growth of the African-American identity; when forged anew it saves, heals and helps define a culture.

The English language belongs first to the whites, and functions sometimes as a weapon, a means of cultural control over slaves. As prelapsarian Adams, whites use language to give names to things, to taxonomize phenomena. African-American slaves were among such phenomena and, as in the case of the first animals, were given names by that force (whites-Adams) with dominion over them. In *Beloved* Mr. Garner, for example, provides Baby Suggs with a name different from that to which she is accustomed, that with which she grew up. "If I was you I'd stick to Jenny Whitlow," he advises her. "Mrs. Baby

Suggs ain't no name for a freed Negro" (Morrison 167). But "Baby Suggs" is not simply an arbitrary appellation. Even the Saussurean might concede that it has more weight as a signifier than "Jenny," since it was, after all, "all she had left of the 'husband' she claimed" (168-9), the husband who gave her the name. Mr. Garner does not merely give Baby Suggs a new name in this case but destroys an existing one. And as a white person, he is legitimated in his nominal act. English is his. This point is encapsulated nicely by Morrison when, after a failed attempt to get himself out of trouble via a clever manipulation of the white language he has learned as a slave, Sixo is chastised by Schoolteacher who "beat him anyway to show him that definitions belonged to the definers not to the defined" (225). And aside from simply naming things, from being the "definers", whites exercise their cultural hegemony to a large extent by means of language. Sethe tells Denver about Schoolteacher's habit of repeatedly asking his slaves questions, and that he would "carry round a notebook and write down what we said". She reasons that "it was them questions that tore Sixo up" (44). Schoolteacher is acting after the fashion of the Englishman Haines in Joyce's *Ulysses*, who is interested in the "Irishness" of Stephen Daedalus only as an anthropologist is interested in, say, the behavior of an aboriginal culture. Language helps Schoolteacher to codify or taxonomize African-Americans into the appropriate strata of animals, which is the hypothesis –that blacks are animals– upon which he beings to interrogate his slaves.

Occasionally, however, an African-American finds it useful to appropriate the English language for his/her own purpose –or weapon– typically as a means to combat, compete with or deceive white persons, although in most cases blacks resent English and feel helplessly foreign to it. For an example of the former, Halle "loved […] the alphabet", Denver tells us. "He could count on paper" (245).

The pun in the phrasal verb "count on" suggests that Halle can both count numbers on paper as well as rely upon the advantages generally afforded by linguistic savvy. Halle's motive, interestingly, is purely self-defense: Denver remembers him saying that "If you can't count they can cheat you", and that "If you can't read they can beat you" (245). Similarly, Ralph Ellison's invisible man perceives language as a means of sleight, as a tool to be used cautiously and defensively:

> I had to be careful though, not to speak too much like a northern Negro; they wouldn't like that. The thing to do, I thought with a smile, was to give them hints that whatever you did or said was weighted with broad and mysterious meanings that lay just beneath the surface. (178)

This case is particularly ironic, since the narrator, in making this decision, will speak neither like a northern nor a southern "Negro", but like a white person. As we shall see, African-American language is characterized by its comparative forthrightness, its immediacy, its unequivocal nature –not by its duplicity. But these two cases are the exception; most African-Americans resent the language to such an extent that they refuse to appropriate it even as a means to arm themselves culturally. One slave fears that book-learning and language would "change his mind –make him forget things he shouldn't and memorize things he shouldn't" (Morrison 245).

The abnegation of black language, it seems, necessitates the abnegation of a black culture that is woven into that language; most African-Americans are not willing to make that sacrifice, or at least they do not think that it will amount to anything. They are pessimistic and concessive in their reception of the use of white English. Sethe remarks that "Schoolteacher was teaching us things we couldn't learn" (226). Baby Suggs, working in the kitchen with Mrs. Gardner, "talked as little as she could get away with because what was there to say that the roots of her tongue could manage?" (166). Most Sweet Home men were allowed "even [to] learn reading if they wanted to –but they didn't want to since nothing important to them could be put down on paper" (147). Sixo even stops speaking English altogether, since "there was not future in it" (30).

THE *BELOVED* LANGUAGE OF TONI MORRISON

If there is no future in white English, then clearly something new must be forged. A linguistic antithesis is necessary if African-American culture is to blossom; it needs a language of its own. In *Beloved* we see the signs of the nascent, growing language. Needless to say, it can be interpreted and explained in a number of different ways, although one may extract three characteristics of this language that, taken together, seem justifiably to represent the scope of its nature as manifested in Morrison's novel. They are its unique relevancy to the African-American experience, its healing properties and its spirituality or mysteriousness.

The African-American language in *Beloved* grows in part out of its serviceable nature, its adaptability to a given crisis or situation. Characters find themselves speaking in a language they scarcely knew they had developed, a language that emerges almost teleologically, as if to help them out of a bind or guide them through sudden hard times. When Paul D. and the slaves to which he is enchained escape from the Georgia prison camp, their success is in large part a result of the common language whereby they collectively sustain themselves, endure the unendurable:

> With a sledge hammer in his hands and Hi Man's lead, the men got through. They sang it out and beat it up, garbling the words so they could not be understood; tricking the words so their syllables yielded up other meanings. They sang the women they knew; the children they had been; the animals they had tamed themselves or

seen others tame. They sang of bosses and masters and misses; of mules and dogs and the shamelessness of life. They sang lovingly of graveyard and sisters long gone. Or pork in the woods; meal in the man; fish on the line; cane, rain and rocking chairs. (128)

The end of this language is not surface-communication: the men "garble" the words with the result that they cannot understand one another. They "trick" the words with the result that the very syllables do not mean what they may have been intended to mean. The key to translation is in the deep structure. Superficially they sing about common ideas such as men and women, bosses, animals, death, eating, weather and furniture. The real import of their speech, however, is fortitude, brotherhood, the excitement and fear they all acknowledge that simultaneously inflame them, propel them as if to an undiscovered country.

Perhaps certain oral traditions are inaugurated on this day of liberation, of the sort the fugitives could teach their children and their children's children. The songs animate them, are forged out of the experience. Paul D. speaks elsewhere of such "songs he knew from Georgia", which "were flat-headed nails for pounding and pounding and pounding" (48). As a newly domesticated father figure, of course, such songs "didn't fit" his new, tamer household life. "They were too loud, had too much power for the little house chores he was engaged in –resetting table legs; glazing" (48). We can see here that certain songs are preferred in certain contexts, which makes sense, seeing that the songs arose directly from experience and inevitably evoke the experiences that begot them. Paul D. the father figure must think of new songs while he lives with Sethe, Denver and Beloved.

Another characteristic of African-American language is related to the first, but more focused in definition: it is that the language has healing properties. Toward the end of the novel, Sethe is spiritually moribund on account of her guilt and inability to completely justify the murder of her daughter. She continues in a downward spiral of despondency until roused by uniquely effective words by the thirty women that come to her rescue:

> For Sethe it was as though the Clearing had come to her with all its heat and simmering leaves, where the voices of the women searched for the right combination, the key, the code, the sound that broke the back of words. Building voice upon voice until they found it, and when they did it was a wave of sound wide enough to sound deep water and knock the pods off chestnut trees. It broke over Sethe and she trembled like the baptized in its wash. (308)

Here we have a sort of meta-language, not unlike that of the escaping prisoners. The meaning of the women's words is not in the words, but in the "key, the code, the sound that broke the back of the words". The women have to come together in a special sort of solidarity; they have to try to speak the words again and again, "building voice upon voice", until finally the signifiers are disabled and the performative, remedial speech is unleashed. And the language is so powerful, stripped of the mere words that have had their "backs broken", that Sethe is veritably "baptized in its wash". She is transformed. We get the sense here that the intervention of a white preacher, using language peculiar to white culture, would not have so exorcised Sethe as these women have done. It would have hung on the air, remained stagnant.

The third and last characteristic of the new tongue is its mysteriousness. Morrison seems deliberately abstract when she conveys certain types of dialogue and communication, as if to suggest that some occurrences of African-American communication are more spiritual than linguistic; that real communication takes place only in the unique confluence a variety of circumstances, including but not limited to language. Denver and Beloved speak in "Sweet, crazy conversations full of half sentences, daydreams and misunderstandings more thrilling than understanding could ever be" (80). "More thrilling than understanding" –Morrison is pressing the idea of a new language, unfettered, as it were, by understanding. She is being comical here, in suggesting that language even has a purpose more important than "understanding". But the idea is that a certain vernacular has arisen out of the exceptionally dreadful conditions of slavery, conceived in unfathomable circumstances and made of the residual power of those circumstances –a power beyond "understanding".

Like the exchange between Denver and Beloved, Sethe and Paul D. experience a sort of mysterious transaction: they share a common history, each interested in "things neither knew about the other – the things neither had word– shapes for [...]" (116). That experience must be powerful, even beyond understanding, for which there are no "word-shapes". There is indeed a significance in these verbal exchanges that seems able to be comprehended only by those who, to some extent, have participated in the circumstances that engendered the new language –great enslavement and dehumanization.

Slavery, a devastating lot, had called for a language powerful enough to confront it –to express it and heal its wounds and grasp its mystery. It was nonsensical to use the language of the master in order to articulate the experience of the enslaved. For this reason Morrison's characters learn a new language, learn to speak on a potent, spiritual level unique to their history.

If white English is the thesis and African-American English the antithesis, we think that the synthesis remains to be discovered; we do not think it is something in which Morrison is pointedly interested in this novel. Perhaps there will arise a language that blends the experiences of both the Euro- and the African-American, and this faithfully, not artificially, so that the history of the one becomes indistinguishable from the history of the other, each with the common end of telling a single, unbroken American story.

LINGUA-CULTURAL BASTARDY IN CE'S *CHILDREN OF KOLOKO*

Chin Ce's fictional narrative of postcolonial Africa, *Children of Koloko*, is manifestly distinctive in purpose. It is a work of satire which also aims at much didacticism, its intent being to correct and point an alternative course. Thus may Chin Ce's fiction be distinguished from the deeply sympathetic intensity of Morrison's *Beloved*.

In a different setting in an African heartland, the characters of Chin Ce's *Children of Koloko* are at odds with their present hybrid traditions. Unlike their African American counterparts, these people are not impeded by the feeling of being uprooted from (cultural) ancestry. Rather they are encumbered by a colonial heritage that contradicts their native wisdom, the symptom of which their use of the English language forms a main part.

Here in Koloko, the ancient language of measured controlled and deliberate wisdom has degenerated by the infusion of new modern life ways that only serve to further alienate the people from their roots. Language becomes a hollow act full of mere pretence and barren innuendos.

We are made to see this earlier in young Yoyo's daydream recollections at Boko; the Americanism he puts on occasionally with his friend Nunu is clearly an act: "What the hell is the old man bossing and hollering for? One of these days were I'm gonna pull him...Dammit!" (26). Its hollowness is underlined by their idle frolicking through foreign magazines, the source of this juvenile fantasy which lasts only briefly. The narrator rightly calls them the "make-believe." (26). Later in Koloko, Fathead also adopts the make-believe to garner some feeling of importance on each return

81

from his "foreign tours". The narrator tells how the rich owner of a multi million naira mansion will publicly dress down his building contractor "adding to it a repertoire of Americanisms, like 'slob,' 'dummy,' and 'bum,' for the benefit of any one around" (76). Vulgar ostentation assumes a foreign import, a materialism of the western arriviste. At the house warming ceremony Fathead declares: "money is an international language" (133), which evidently makes purchase of an assortment of English, French, German, Swedish and Russian wines a simple act of generosity. It is the language of satire which grows progressively as "Fathead bows in the European fashion"(133) in the usual imitation of his mentors.

The language of this fictional Nigerian village is in sharp contrast to the language of the black people of Morrison's novel. The ebullient narrator in *Children of Koloko is* constrained by the changing order of living: his language combines African sensitivities and western modernity with often despairing consequences. For instance, the dialogue between Yoyo and Kata is tinged with rustic inflections, reflecting the rural sentiment of the old woman that has always been there in the cultural background of the entire story. Kata deftly maneuvers the discussion and starts out with folk benignity, or a pretension of such: "It will be good for you...and him too" (42), she begins. Kata is about to recast history, a past in which she had seen better days and played "noble" roles toward her one-time ward, Fathead. She does this with native cunning and sense of the dramatic which elicit amusement: "She made a face, rubbed her stubby nose, and spat through tobacco-stained teeth. Little Ada recoiled in horror"(45). To young Yoyo's mind her laughter "was very much like the hyena's" while her tactics reminds him of the "old tortoise" (42) she was. During the chat Kata describes Fathead whom we have now learnt was her one-time ward, as "a true son of the land who knows how to look after old people" (42), and talking about joint pains she says "I feel like someone bashed thoroughly with a pestle" (43). Her plaintive solicitation at the rich man's quarters is a trickster's act cast in traditional badinage: "It's my waist-o! I have no money…" (44).

Even in expletives which are but further symptoms of this deterioration of language art, Kata's curses induce descriptive distortions of physical qualities. To her observation, Mabelle, Fathead's stepmother walks "baka baka as if…" (47) and Lukeman whom Yoyo claims bought all his pears on credit is a "drink-and-fall-by-the-gutter oaf" (41). Kata calls Abeze "husband beater" (52) in bipartite insult on the woman for her intractability –"big and belligerent"– and on Old Bap's (her brother's) seeming lack of power to tame his shrew wife, Abeze.

The names of people in Koloko locale are similarly distorted. Characters take on a new name from an illiterate distortion of the phonetic: the train is "turan" (46) for Kata; or from what is clearly semi-literate or broken assimilation of the white man's language: "inconveniences" is "inconsequency" even for missionary-educated Obeku (Old Bap) whose English is said to be "nearest the Queen's" (88). "Reputation" is "repudiate" for JJC who also says "lest" instead of "let's," (64-67) etc.

The image of Big Mam's, described as a "huge tree-trunk of laps" (49) calls the tropical baobab to mind. "In those days," the narrator says "she only had to bark once to send the bravest fellow behind the mask tearing away in disregard of his own dignified presence" (52). The cultural inversion of a masked spirit (masquerade) backing up in fear of a human is a strong indicator of the grandmother's (read this African village's) legendary power ironically dwindled or diminished over time. Now her barking would only confirm an old proverb that said "a barking dog would never bite you" (52). Most or every expression in a traditional or modern sense goes to suggest that the majority of the citizens of Koloko society are now less effectual in character and training than their grandparents had been in times past. Tuma who always begins his story with a reference to those old times is fond of saying: "Nowadays elders no longer teach the young ones or show befitting examples…and so we young men have not learned from them"(96).

By the use of nicknames, language in Koloko society grows progressively hollow. Nicknames in place of actual names of persons is laughter on a recent tradition of title taking, a phenomenon of cultural bastardies in the growing modernity where no one queried how anyone built his/her financial empire. Fante Ayadu is the real name of Fathead, the nickname referring to his figure which looks like "a man-size caterpillar standing on its tail" (72). Yoyo's father is Foreman Obeku but every child affectionately calls him Bap. Big Mam is Abeze –the term of Big Mam referring both to her size and her position as grandmother in the family just as elder Obeku himself, the narrator's grandfather is called Old Bap. Chief Dogomutun had taken on the ridiculous title of Dogkiller because he liked the "the manner of high pitch and long drawn voice" by which his political tout called the sobriquet after he had killed "six dogs with three shots" (34) of his gun. A gun wielding politician does not seem uncommon in local politics. Later he is described as a "good for nothing politician" (166) by a member of the press corps for bagging a jail term. Before his jail term Dogomutun is reported to have confessed he would "drink palm wine through the nose while making the million with his fingers" (162), in a language of traditional myth making that suggests the deeper import that the chief is either drunk and therefore mentally unstable all the time or earns his way through some other equally dubious means.

Where there are praise names they merely serve the purpose of ridicule. In addition, other praise names are concocted by admirers and fawners like Okon and Ade with such lavish descriptiveness as "young multi-millionaire-in-Koloko-and-beyond", "shining star", etc. Okon himself is nicknamed the Billy and the title had stuck to his name like the real thing. The three boys like to think of Okon as "parrot and woodpecker" in one (82), suggesting that Okon, like most other Koloko townsmen, is worth only talkative or noise value. Dickie says of him, using a lexical pun to denote the smooth fakery of the local cheerleader, "He's too warm and that's how he worms his way..." (82).

Unlike in Achebe's novels which celebrate the staid and germane dignity of oral art through proverbs, here in Koloko there are no such elevations of thought and mastery of traditional eloquence. There are little or no incidents for proverbs, and the lack of them points to the general diminution of African values in Koloko. Although Mika had glibly remarked: "all of us come from one father. Same father Lokoko who gave birth to she who gave birth to another" (130), there is no elaborate detail or legend of ancestry that in local tradition would serve to bind the people with a feeling of tribal oneness, a sense of shared obligations and loyalty. Such is the bane of this traditional society that some distortions of Christian creation story emerge in their legend of ancestry. Kiza elaborates upon a story about Koloko's perennial seasons of frivolity and says: "Our ancestor, Lokoko, was said to have clowned before God on the night of creation and when the good Lord gave him a gigantic pot he broke it into pieces" (165).

Kiza further tells his listeners that "out of the rubble emerged a minstrel who vowed his descendants would forever make his neighbours happy with the sound of laughter in their ears" (165). Making neighbors happy is euphemism for the English idiom of becoming the laughing stock of the community. Thus as the new language of this African society deteriorates with westernizing sophistication, use of proverbs remains sparse, just as with Africa's economic poverty and social deprivation, ancient heritage or culture can be thrown overboard. The classic example is the statement by Mika the palm wine dealer at the house opening ceremony of the political stalwart: "A hungry man does not waste his time on proverbs when the real meal is before him" (133).

Fathead, chief celebrant, had earlier told his audience "gbata-gbata is a language that has two faces: it might mean good, it might mean disaster" (131), and is rather proud that his particular *gbata-gbata* (author does not provide translation but we might deduce this to mean a rally) holds good tidings of the culinary kind which the people rather enjoyed. Amanda Grants mentions the abuse of tradition in Fathead's two proverbs. "In this drama of social and communal acquiescence, tradition is made culprit," she notes, and rightly adds that all those men and women who applaud Fathead "are unlike their modern enlightened liberated counterparts who acquiesce to the impoverishment of their nation state so long as it carves for them a niche of the social table" (17).

Yoyo himself thinks that Fathead had chosen to declare a public feast and should be held responsible for the rowdiness at his homestead. "Was it not he who declared a feast and the lizards came calling?" (145). This is in reference to a traditional Igbo proverb that says a man who brings in ant-infested faggots to his compound should naturally expect the visit of lizards. Yoyo knows this proverb but does not execute it well enough. It is artfully explored by Achebe in his works *Arrow of God*: Ezeulu, scolding his wife who resents and blames him for their son's outrageous act against the sacred python, says to her: "You must be telling me in your mind that a man who brings home ant-infested faggots should not complain if he is visited by lizards. You are right" (59). He is to use this proverb again in an argument with his friend while pointing out that the responsibility for disunity of the tribe laid with the traitors among the people and not him who had only chosen to send one of his sons to learn the white man's ways.

> ...white men would not have overrun entire Olu and Igbo if we did
> not help them. Who showed them the way to Abame? ...So let
> nobody come to me now and complain that the white man did this
> and did that. The man who brings in ant-infested faggots into his hut
> should not grumble when lizards begin to pay him a visit. (132)

Ironically the same proverb is used later again against Ezeulu himself,[1] which proves traditional Igbo belief in self-responsibility, or the imperative to pin-point the root of a vexatious problem. But the general paucity of proverb use in Koloko village is a good indication that the new-agers of Koloko have lost some of Africa's finest traditions. In their quest for social notability or relevance under the white man's laws and standards to the exclusion or neglect of their own values, this loss comes as no real surprise.

The satire on 'General' Dickie and his 'madness' is symptomatic of the psychic disorder of African leaders in modern society –a theme amply illustrated in all the Koloko stories. Here the language is typical of the narrator's jaunty, deprecatory attitude towards his people and all their affairs:

> What looked like a joke soon became a matter of communal
> embarrassment when Dickie began to prevent people from passing
> the road that ran through his frontage to the market square. How
> dared they pass the street without saluting General Dickie? he
> barked.(179)

One may contrast this with Yoyo's earlier wishes for a compassionate distancing from his community and may wonder exactly what this language and attitude of inconsistency in the hero-narrator could hold for his society.

Dora was reclining on the sofa next to Bap's avoiding every body's eyes with placid disinterest. Dora was so much like my Mam. Always keeping her opinions to herself, she surpassed even the holy Mary. Unknown to her, Dora had given me a clue as to the new attitude to hold for these sons and daughters of Koloko. (177)

It may be conceded that at this point of the hero's return to native land there is a subtle change in his attitude to his people. But this attitude of goodwill which the Koloko hero claims to give his people could also mean one of defeat or indifference. It can be witnessed here in Yoyo's treatment of his old chum recuperating in a psychiatric home:.

> Dickie ... merely looked at me as I gripped his hand in a parting greeting.
> 'See you around, guy,' I told him.
> 'Yeah, Catch you in the next life,' Dickie replied. (182)

And along the way a mischievous idea that Dickie is paying a price for killing chickens in cold blood dominates the hero's thoughts.

We have to look back to the village meeting of Koloko for some reminder of a tradition of oratorical elegance often celebrated in tribal life. But here too this eloquence comes in snatches. For instance, Foreman Obeku's familiar line of argument is delivered through a reconstruction of one of the numerous tortoise legends.

> 'Tortoise brought new woman to the clan and for reasons known to him, warned all his randy boys, "let no one touch even a scale of her body!"
> 'Every one in the clan obeyed father tortoise and avoided the newest young and beautiful member like a caste --that is, not touching a scale of her body.' (103)

Legends form a major aspect of West African folklore. And as Okpewho argues, folklore is more than just the "literary aspect of what the folk do" (4). In other words, it is the world view and life of traditional Africa. Hearing the learned teacher Foreman Obeku (Bap) relay some of the old tales, we experience the pale, flickering world of the past again. In any case it enlivens the discourse and aptly seals the verdict –even if a misguided one– against the elders at the village meeting.

Apart from Obeku, Yoyo's father, whose eloquence is apparent by his use of the trickster story to condemn the elders for Koloko's problems, we can see in the women, represented by Aina their leader, real matriarchal power over anti-social behaviours. Again this is almost a forgotten heritage. Nevertheless her oral rhetoricism contrasts sharply with the narrator's (Yoyo's) own abrupt "point-blank" narrative.

> 'The elders have spoiled the village!' her voice was no-nonsense and point-black, 'because they lost the wisdom to teach their young who look up to them.
> 'What happens when the nanny is chewing her cud?' she barked.
> 'The tender ones are watching the rhythm of her mouth!' came the women's chorus. This was followed by a roar of applause among them while our mesmerised men could only watch. Da Aina raised her aims revealing her flabby Christian mother's muscles and there was quietness again in the seated assembly.' (102)

In spite of this community dialogue, *Children of Koloko* as a modern narrative creates an English that is incongruous for tribal or communal expressions. This sad displacement or consequent loss of the traditional "beloved" language of yore does not leave all hopes lost. There are still the likes of Aina and Foreman Obeku through whom the African society may continue to hand forth its fount of traditional aesthetics even as the younger generation, embodied in Ce's narrator, gropes for direction.

CONCLUSION

Chin Ce's and Toni Morrison's worlds are clearly at opposite divides in spite of common ancestral depths. While Toni Morison's novel seeks to demonstrate that the African-American culture is capable of creating its own mystifying meaning out of the language of the white masters, it seems to be Ce's idea that in a modern African environment where progress is equated with vulgar western civilization, African language, culture and tradition are doomed to the desert of aridity and suffocation.

The English language of the *Koloko* stories may not be a variation of Standard English. The stories point to a near- if not total loss of heritage; they seem to suggest that the language we witness in the older novels of Achebe has been, like the modern states of Africa years after independence, lost in an emerging adolescent modernity. One is no less in agreement with its introductory statements that Ce's particularity on "the drift of his generation, in harmony with the thematic bent of the entire work is (much more than) a sardonic humour"(14). Chin Ce reassesses a heritage that is becoming trivialized by "those persons whose lives, in their entirety, are no more serious" (14) than the colloquialism of the language of narrative. Morrison celebrates a new black just as Ce is critical of the new African tradition.

NOTE

[1] This time Nwaka uses the proverb against Ezeulu, his rival, when he says: "a man who brings in ant-ridden faggots into his hut should expect the visit of lizards. But if Ezeulu is telling us that he is tired of the white man's friendship our advice to him should be: *You tied the knot, you should also know how to undo it...*" Again the lesson here is on taking responsibility for every action no matter how trifle it may seem.

WORKS CITED

Achebe, Chinua. *Arrow of God*. Ibadan:Heinemann, 1989.

Ce, Chin. *Children of Koloko*. Handel International Edition. Morrisville: Lulu Press, 1992.

Ellison, Ralph. *Invisible Man*. Second Vintage International Ed. New York: Random House, 1995.

Grants, Amanda. "Memory, Transition and Dialogue: The Cyclic Order of Chin Ce's Oeuvres" *Journal of African Literature and Culture* No.3, 2006. 11-29.

Joyce, James. *Ulysses*. Everyman's Library Edition. Alfred A Knopf: New York, 1992.

Morrison, Toni. *Beloved*. Vintage International Edition. New York: Random House, 2004.

Okpewho, Isidore. *African Oral Literature: Backgrounds, Character, and Continuity* Indiana: Indiana University Press 1992.

5

The Postcolonial Dialogue

OF CHIN CE'S *GAMJI COLLEGE*

GMT Emezue

*U*sing Chin Ce's book of fiction *Gamji College* this paper attempts to compare the postcolonial argument in African literature with the novels of Chinua Achebe and that of his younger compatriot Chin Ce who represents the vocal generation of younger African writers. The voice of this generation rings with far more disturbing notes through the current arguments that embrace issues of environment, citizenship and leadership in Africa. We shall try to prove that Chin Ce extends the post-colonial dialogue to modern citizenship issues by noting how citizenship perception of a whole history, or the lack of it, affects the liberationist potential of the contemporary nation state.

Chin Ce employs the literary art as a discourse of alternative realities or options where the heroes or protagonists of his fiction are not casting about and failing in their attempts at their heroic expectations, as in previous examples of Chinua Achebe, but active challengers of the status quo offering a rigorous dialogue for the individual reader to discard conflicting and constricting paradigms in his redefinition of his place in society.

THE POSTCOLONIAL NOVEL IN AFRICA

In her criticism against the obsession of black South African novelists with analysing the corruption in their societies instead of resolving the fate of these societies in terms of profound social change, Nadine Gordimer did show hasty judgement when she concluded that '...the postcolonial political novel like the political novel of the colonial struggle seems scarcely to have scratched the surface of the African situation.' (qtd. in Ogungbesan vii) On the contrary the postcolonial literatures *did* investigate Africa's political and social dilemmas with much more than a fleeting concern and, where necessary, articulated a resolution that has profound social implications for individual and collective existence.

It is rather by drawing from other such generalisations as Gordimer's that the major concern of post colonial studies in literature seems to have become a fad of 'talking' or 'writing back', a fixation on ideological revisionism, sometimes within the context of racial or gender inscriptions, rather than on internal development issues of once colonised societies of Africa. This informed the tendency to continue the reading of Achebe's *Things Fall Apart* as a talk-back to Conrad's (and Cary's) 'preposterous and perverse'[1] portraiture of the black man in such European novels on Africa as *Heart of Darkness* (and *Mister Johnson*). This approach has tended to dominate postcolonial literary studies particularly by Western college departments of literature[2] when a better option would rather have been, borrowing Ogungbesan's words, 'in the variety of methods with which (these writers) have interpreted contemporary realties and proposed their own visions of the future' (viii).

For Nigeria, a creation of Britain, its postcolonial condition has given rise to a wealth of literatures 'profoundly influenced by politics,' which Bernth Lindfors once argued were 'shaped by the same forces that have transformed much of the African continent during the past hundred years.' And this probably explains why their works, as Lindfors remarked, 'reflect and project the course of Africa's cultural revolution' (135). For Nigerian, and indeed African writing, this revolution began with Chinua Achebe's *Things Fall Apart* and crystallises with contemporary (such as Chin Ce's) interrogation of present contexts with an even deeper sense of foreboding for the future.

CE'S POSTCOLONIAL DIALOGUE

Few modern fictions of Africa have raised doubts concerning Africa's nation states and their future generations as have Chin Ce's Gamji and Koloko[3] stories. Chin Ce's consistently echoes the question Davidson asks in *Black Man's Burden*, a questioned posed by Africa's literati to policy makers of the nation states:

> why... adopt models from those very countries or systems that have oppressed and despised you? Why not modernise from the models of your own history, or invent new models? (19)

This question is at the heart of the three issues that dominate Ce's fiction and some of his early poetry: the commitment to and awareness of the environment, the testing of its notions on the scale of communal good and hindsight from past history, and the artist's response to this test being the rejection of unwholesome, even if popular, paradigms that paralyse or constrain genuine social transformation.

Achebe had argued for an engaging form of artistic diligence that distinguishes African literature from its western counterpart. In his opinion, an adequate revolution for me to espouse (is) ...to help my society regain belief in itself and put away the complexes of the years of denigration and selfabasement. And it is essentially a question of education, in the best sense of that word. (44)

Similar ideas of the artiste's responsibility in African postcolonial settings have predominated the discourse of Ce's fiction and essays. In his critique of the Nigerian state, Ce argues that the degeneration of social educational and cultural standards is the result of political and economic chaos entrenched by colonially inherited structures and poorly assimilated traditions.

At forty Nigeria today, with especially such distended bellies of present-day democracy as Olusegun Obasanjo and company steering her, actually fit the above description of gargantuan folly. The political foppery of unimaginative minds emerging president and lawmakers has become the country's recurring theme in the drama of its own undoing. ('Bards' 8)

Earlier in his treatise Chin Ce had remarked that "the development of Nigeria seems to be all talk and little progress" and asked: "with the obvious lacunae of imaginative thinking is it surprising at the vacuity of their leadership and at modern Nigeria's descent into an African redundancy syndrome?" (4). Ce's criticism of Nigeria is behoved from the extent of neocolonial destabilisation of indigenous society and the imposition of structures that perpetuate this destabilisation to the continued advantage of imperial powers. It is probably what Fanon meant when he states:

the violence which has ruled over the ordering of the colonial world, which has ceaselessly drummed the rhythm for the destruction of native social forms..., that same violence will be claimed and taken over by the native at the very moment ...he enters into forbidden (colonial) quarters. (31)

Because they were merely co-opted by their masters, opting to remain in the neo-colonial 'closet' and accepting 'being silenced and dismissed as marginal', (Weiss 11) the local lackeys that bestride the political administration of modern nation states of Africa are unwilling to implement a program of restructuring that will return power to the indigenous base from which the tribal societies had been rocked in the first place. Of the subjugation of minority tribes at the hands of foreign powers who for centuries fashion the economic and technological programmes that stifle their existence, Deloria Jnr, the Sioux Indian intellectual argues that with the continual threat of co-optation facing minority groups,

> ... it is imperative that the basic sovereignty of the minority group be recognised in order that racial minorities may be placed in a negotiating position as a group and which would eventually nullify cooptation. (113)

Deloria Jnr also parallels the Red Indian situation with black people's struggle for power negotiation in America through the emergence of the sense of community which must 'continue to struggle for justice' in a racially oppressive environment where 'minorities are 'just as invisible' as the invisible poor in Michael Harrington's *The Other America* (106).

For the committed African intellectual he too is involved in a struggle analagous to that of his kindred in America, a dialogue which requires a constant reappraisal of the African social reality through the rigorous intellectual engagement embraced by modern African writers and philosophers. In the words of Asouzu; "there is need at all times for this critical stance because in addressing fundamental philosophical issues the philosopher (–artist) relies on the ambience provided by his world...."(18).

Ce's novels reaffirm the argument that colonial entrenchments in the native state still hold African nationalities in servitude and these un-dethroned legacies structures have guaranteed the emergence of inept leaderships around the continent. The role of the artist is therefore seen in the context of not only challenging this condition but also constantly reappraising society's progress and rejecting held notions that limit the potential of the underdeveloped world.

In the Gamji stories such a role is aptly filled by Tai, the protagonist of the first part. As a first-year entrant to Gamji College (representing the so-called democratic Nigerian nation state) his outlook offers us an objective appraisal of degenerating educational structures seen in the dilapidated and unkempt environment of the once-towering Gamji institute.

> Dangerous gully erosion, like a predatory monster, had lashed through the only motorway. How was such innocent course of nature allowed to become a menacing beast? … the neat drainage of Gamji College caved into wide gullies threatening the very foundation of the college. The hostels stank abominably and with each gust of wind came the horrible ooze of filth. (4-5)

Tai's narrative consciousness prepares our mind for the subsequent loss of faith in the generation that patterns after colonial fripperies while still suffering by its ignorance and stubborn refusal to give them up. The vestige of religious proselytising (symbolic of the dangling Christian cross whipped at that precarious angle by the elements) indicates the imbalance of the post-colonial situation. The suggestion of imbalance continues from here through the second and third parts –in the symbolic other-world experience of Milord, and the unusually large head of young Nap that had given his mother a terrible time giving birth to him. These techniques of signification prod us to appreciate the

98

ironic situation that while Gamji College deteriorates, the president is on a visit passing through but stops by at the behest of his nephew the rector of the institute. For president Baba Sonja it was an occasion to repeat 'the time-worn phrase he uses to explain the 'numerous failures of his government' (19), an occasion for the usual political gerrymandering and public chicanery of Nigerian political leaders. In his religious motivation to tinker with the national anthem lies a cosmetic attempt at nation building if not an entirely misguided one.

> Baba Sonja had given his nationals a new national anthem reconstructed from an old martial doggerel but which now put Sonja's God in the centre-spread of the national map:
> *Arise children of El-Shaddai*
> *God's holy call obey...* (18-19)

Religious fervour engendered by the new democracy is indicative of the religious divide through which the colonial legacy had partitioned Africa. The post-colonial state is structured after the messianic arrogance that drove the colonial invasion and exploitation of Africa and, in the minds of the invaders, legitimised the plunder of her natural resources. This messianic aggression, suggestive of a deep psychic and spiritual derailment, is evident in not only the tyrannical president of the Gamji nation but in their mass of followers. Chin Ce exposes such blind following in the sycophancy of Gamji citizens who support and actually carry out Sonja's directive for spiritual cleansing of the nation state, a problematic contract even for the Christian god if we consider that it is the politics of Baba Sonja and his deteriorating educational institutions that actually need cleansing.

> "Alright, some other time. But we'll pray for you, okay?
> "Pray for me?"

"Well, you'll pray with us, isn't that fair?"

The prayer lasted twelve minutes during which Brother James earnestly reminded God his promise not to abandon any of his prodigal children in the wilderness of sin and damnation. And if God had forgotten, there were copious passages in His Holy Book to recall His mind to that solemn promise. But it appeared there was one beloved who (gibbering and babbling interspersed) stood at the great risk of going to hell fire. As a result, he was now seizing the power which God had bestowed upon him –the power of casting and binding both here and in heaven– to loosen the shackles and send the agents of darkness into the bottomless pit... [names of some imagined secret cults were reeled off in a spell]. (28-29)

Such a prayer during the transitional phase of African societies would show a blend of traditional animist humility with that of an emboldened confidence in the façade of a loving Christian god –a merger of traditional complaisance and European coercive tactics. Mary's prayer in Achebe's *No Longer At Ease* in direct speech demonstrates this:

'Oh God of Abraham, God of Isaac and God of Jacob,' she burst forth, 'the Beginning and the End. Without you we can do nothing. The great river is not big enough for you to wash your hands in. You have the yam and you have the knife; we cannot eat unless you cut us a piece. We are like ants in your sight. We are like little children who only wash their stomach when they bath leaving their back dry...' (8)

Chin Ce's treatment of Brother James's prayer concurs with the psycho-social reality of modern Nigeria where nationhood had ossified with years of military plunder and acts of executive lawlessness by its civilian governments. The doctrinaire religious zeal of the new nationals when contrasted with the transitional society represented in Chinua Achebe's second novel *No Longer at Ease* cannot but show marked evidence that the modern state quite like its earlier traditional phase is clearly in an even greater danger –something uncannily similar to what is currently witnessed in the monopoly and arrogance of power exhibited by some western leaders in contemporary global politics. The second part of the Gamji story ('The Cross') prepares us finally for the rejection of this alternative. It is foreshadowed in Part I by Tai's loss of patience with his proselytising band of friends who much like the colonial missionary are intent on co-opting him to their fold against his finer wishes.

> James and Peter had slithered to his bedside to rouse him up from a midday nap. It was this part that made him very angry.
> "We hope there will be no other excuses today...." they laughed uneasily -a fixed dry laughter that bore no more warmth than the sound of their voices....For a moment Tai was thrown completely by what was clearly a preemptive strike. But he tried to summon some wit. These brothers certainly had a lot of unflattering traits. (31-32)

This face-off reveals the truth underlying both sides, the one a descendant of well-meaning but quite destructive colonial missionaries and the other a restive and independent African mind. This rejection is like a clearing of fields and continues in the second part where Jerry discovers, to his little amazement anyway, that his political associate comrade Nap is as irremediably plunged in the violence and brigandage of power mongering as most of his other opponents. 'The Gun' story here is equally predicated upon a worsening postcolonial problem of power sharing. Western democracy in Africa endangers the populace with its winner-takes-all structure that has seen African countries successively impaled in fratricidal violence and wanton struggles for control of the centre which is particularly Nigeria's major problem as a failed experiment today. Only a few decades earlier in the Ibo nation from which Chin Ce takes his kinship, the pre-colonial traditional society's republican outlook offered a valid and stable organisational structure than what the colonial arrangement enforced upon the people. The Nigerian historian Onwubiko parallels political organisation in Iboland with the 'assembly of Athenian citizens in ancient Greece' (where) every grown up male had the right to air his views on a matter under discussion... and decisions were reached not by voting but by a consensus'(105). While traditional consensual consultation replaced arbitrary colonial imposition by 'local British administrators who were completely ignorant of the structure of indigenous societies' (263), the western-educated elite foisted this ignorance to far worse dimensions. In refusing to restructure the colonial creation of the imperial lords in Africa the local inheritors of the created states forged more atrocious structures of corruption, exploitation and misappropriation of public resources. Political party formation and administration retained its familiar chicanery of violence and brutality. As leaders of Africa try their hands at electioneering, issues that immediately engage them are those of the palate (money and booze), of ethnicity and political irredentism seen here in Gamji politicking:

> "Hey, who is your candidate, man?"
> "Yes. Declare your stand! Are you Yusuf or are you Napoleon?!" (Laughter)
> "Alternatively, are you north or are you south?"
> "Eastern power or western vanguard?"
> "No, he must be of the minority. Can't you see his moustache and ridiculous pipe?" (94-95)

The seed of violent confrontation is sown in a bizarre

interaction of competing interests. Napoleon, late contender and pretender to a progressive alternative while manipulating some members of his tribe, has a gun stowed away to guarantee some advantage over more articulate opponents. Ege ends up as victim of that advantage. Significantly Napoleon's dressing is ominously evocative of the other face of military interventionism in post-colonial Africa's political process and the mentality of the civilian surrogates that imitate it.

> Dressed in rough battle gears and imitation camouflage uniform, his dark sunglasses strapped over his eyes and what looked like a wooden rifle hanging from his waist, Napoleon reeled off revolutionary slogans text after text. Why the hell he was wasting time especially now the familiar, ominous noises of boredom were becoming very audible among the audience (even a deaf could hear?) no one could tell. Napoleon was not yet done. He was like the cock strutting with exaggerated sense of its size. (84)

Rancorous competition for power and control of Gamji union seat which soon degenerates to violence is an echo of Achebe's earlier thesis of power and struggle in *A Man of the People*, his third novel of a postcolonial state which omens of political failure have been witnessed all over West Africa: Nigeria, Liberia, Senegal and Cote d' Voire. In *A Man of the People* Chief Nanga is a public servant cast in the gregarious mould of President Baba Sonja, the Machiavellian prince whose nation states are but principalities acquired in order to rule over their people by the force of arms or the manipulation of others; by their conquering might, or by their fortune or valour (*Prince* 5). As postcolonial African leaders their smooth easy manners mask a determination to perpetuate their claws on power to the ultimate disfavour of their people. In their activities these leaders are no different from their counterparts in pre-colonial tribal warring over land or in 'the intrusive slave raiding and violent activities of the 19th century' (Asouzu 259). Very much in the manner of colonial district officers, President Baba Sonja is like contemporary Nigerian leaders who would manipulate social events to hold out themselves as objects of admiration in the eyes of other less than discerning religious fanatics. The bogey threatens initially to hold Jerry himself under the spell the herd syndrome. But jolted by the political beating of one of the contestants, Ege, Jerry's humanism snaps him out of the deceit The tendency to snuff out the opposition (powerful only by the superiority of ideas than by control of instruments of brutality) is the survival tactic of tyrants and dictators that have blighted the face of Africa and the rest of humanity. Nigerian poet and dramatist Wole Soyinka in his prison notes recalls the incident that gave birth to the title of his prison notes: *The Man Died*

> The dog of this immediate death was a journalist, Segun Sowemimo. He was brutally beaten, he and other colleagues, by soldiers on the orders of a Military Governor of the West. The reason? An imagined slight. But at least he was fortunate –to start with. He had the help of his trade union and as his condition worsened, the Governor was compelled ...to fly him to England for treatment. But gangrene had set in and the affected leg had to be amputated...(23)

Segun Sowemimo later dies of his injury. In *Gamji College*, Ege dies from political beating by jealous opponents. For Jerry, following his monologic progress in understanding his society, it was the beginning of his moments of decision.

> It made the voting and counting event of Thursday a sad one ..., thinking about Ege. He wished Ege would win the presidency.

> But would he survive the ordeal? Jerry wore a serious frown throughout the day. It was a frown that would follow him throughout his stay in Gamji. (111)

Finally Jerry's review of his political involvement or service is a resignation from active connivance (which the likes of the Gamji college registrar and rector are vicarious partakers) in disorganising the constituted process for immediate narrow gains.

Thus the inability of the British and French creations in Africa to become a truly nation state, a theme which Chin Ce continually grapples with, may not be laid entirely at the doorsteps of their leaders. In fact his essay 'Bards and Tyrants' while agreeing with his compatriot's position that 'the trouble with Nigeria is simply and squarely a failure of leadership' (*Trouble* 1) also argues that 'Nigerians seem to pitch their tents with exactly those elements that precipitate corruption and unleash a running spate of havoc in their national life' (21). There Chin Ce states, and it seems convincing enough in *Gamji College* also, that

> Evidently the power-hungry elite do not long for a revolution of the society. It knows that Nigerian masses are not cut in the cloak of their counterparts of the French revolution. All they long for is a rehabilitation of their appetite for indulgence through the return of their own man to government, which seems the only fastest avenue for all coveted wealth. (21-22)

'THE BOTTLE'

The Gamji story Part Two set in a rowdy crowded corner of the village pub ironically called 'New Generation' makes mockery of the ability of the younger generation of Nigerian youths to articulate liberating ideas about nationhood and citizenship. Its social ethic is all 'to the glory of the green bottle' as inscribed in the pub. Thus the three youths tend, in the words of Amanda

Grants, to 'foreshadow a general communal retardation most poignant in (Chin Ce's)…Koloko and Gamji fictions' (11). Grants rightly sees Chin Ce's works as one consistent 'movement in the major characters from one of social preoccupation to that of psychological transition in awareness and growth' (11).

In Grants's 'tripartite' delineation of the progressive order of Chin Ce's writings Dogo, Femi and Milord would represent the northern, western, and eastern divides in which the Nigerian nation was constituted by the colonial British. But the sense of unity and tolerance that had eluded the ethnicities is achieved here in the story where the three collaborators form a camaraderie of wit and jocular humour, and the participants, as if in a game of chance, take turns at poking fun at one another. Dogo takes the dart at him in good faith when Femi taunts his Muslim religious practice of putting their women in seclusion.

> Milord: You know you surprise me, Dogo, how most licentious and sacrosanct at the same time you really act. Dogo made an impatient movement. "You're talking about something you know little about."
> "You think so," sneered Femi. "Now count how many daughters of this land –so much for eve though," he muttered under his breath. "Now count the many daughters of our soil you have wasted in your purdah for their whole life … that's criminal you know?" (56)

The entry of Churchill to join the triad is an extension of their bohemian exuberance. Churchill's' high sounding discoveries of the A and D syndrome of Africa's petty tyrants is in keeping with the inherited structure of Africa's post-colonial dilemma. Easily the intellectual of the four it is little wonder that the rigorous narcissism of his debate is dismissed with the charge of political idle philosophising.

Femi jeered at Churchill. "Now we have another modification of a political propaganda," and Dogo laughed as if vindicated. "What did you expect? The philosopher has been idle since the holiday." (62)

Exit Churchill to let the triad continue their drinking and smoking, the consequence of which we have been intimated is Milord's occasional fractured memory or near loss of consciousness. His occasional unfocussed or sightless vacancy points to a vacuity among youths who hold no positive image of their society.

> Desperate and panicky, Milord tried to rouse himself without success. In that instant time appeared to stand very still and objects motionless. And out of the haziness of his vision came a strange fellow riding a four legged creature in slow motion, a youth very much like himself except he had on a strange part on his head like some extraction from the remote past. ..None of his features seemed discernible. Only the smile: a broad open-mouthed chasm that yawned into eternity. (49)

The preternatural image of the young man (Milord's alter-ego) like a gothic past life contraption which makes Milord resolute against sleep suggests that the youth are losing out. In this case the writer's warning is indeed prophetic as the complete degeneration of Africa's national universities to cult hostage-syndrome becomes a testament of this general national debauchery. Says Chin Ce again in his criticism of the nation state:

> ...where high-ranking society's leaders are either members or founders and patrons of campus cults... (t)he social impact of degenerate education in Nigeria ... (takes) its toll by the high incidence of unemployed graduates, the collapse of its

economy and the erosion of cultural values. (12)

When finally the three youths make their move as last ones to leave the bar at well over midnight, their exit leaves an uneasy warning of the consequences of youth befuddled of vision and lacking a clear direction in spite of its natural endowment.

> The rest ...followed suit, tidying the contents of their glasses. Then they all rose to their feet with slow deliberate movements like a committee of dons on convocation procession. ...
> "Yeah, gentlemen it's been a grand frolic," Dogo recapped in a slow drawl, nodding to Sammy who, stretching and yawning, was dutifully seeing them to the door. (71)

As the writer's warning resonates through the looming collapse of postcolonial educational structures that impair African development, it affirms what Achebe had observed that the artist as a visionary, like his traditional counterpart, must remain in constant moral exchange with members of his society who may choose to neglect the voice of their writers to the eventual peril of the entire superstructure.

CONCLUSION

Read as a postcolonial dialogue, *Gamji College* heavily indicts state power/ citizenship structures. Chin Ce reaffirms the collegiate indebtedness which Oguzie observes of the writer in a post-colonial situation:

> the writer as a member of his society , should show awareness of specific social situations. He is expected to convey historical and social truths, moreover, for taking part in the issues of his times, he may make pronouncements on questions of social and political importance. (160)

Thus where Achebe's novels, in the words of Hamilton, 'appear to demand (yet always seem to fail to deliver) a singular leader of the people' (130), Chin Ce invests the social structure with responsibility for either its retardation or redemption. And where Obi Okonkwo of *No Longer at Ease* and Odili of *A Man of the People* are products of the social realism of Achebe's artistic world view, Chin Ce's characters, by their choices and actions in defence of personal and public ethics, seem to aim at a possible transformation of consciousness. The asymmetrical interaction of creation and creator is made evident in these leaders and citizens who are engaged in the making or marring of the progressive movement toward the reorganisation of the postcolonial state.

It seems therefore that, for Chin Ce the poet-novelist, the modern state does not need heroes, but teachers; is sorely in need of wider paradigms which are being offered here by the moral leverage of characters who can distinguish between narrow interests from public good. Stephen Watts commenting on Plato's vision in *The Republic* notes that "indeed this call to clear away the confused nonsense of current beliefs and to start out fresh from principle has occurred rather frequently in human history" (xvi). Art has been a useful tool directed to fulfil a reader's quest for the meaning of existence, and, for a beleaguered people, to point out an alternative path to some pragmatic reinterpretation of social reality.

NOTES

[1]Achebe's paper "An Image of Africa" published in the *Massachusett Review* (1977) sparked the first serious indictment of western stereotypes of Africa in European novels.

[2]IRCALC editors, in their introduction to the *Journal of African Literature and Culture*, (JALC) *No. 3*, 2006 volume, comment on 'a good number of 'post-colonial' discourses that appear to fascinate Western college departments of African literature.'

[3]Chin Ce's first published fiction, *Children of Koloko* (2001), is a satire about post colonial African village caught in the euphoria of modernisation with its attendant neglect of the environment and lack of direction on the part of its leaders and youth.

WORKS CITED

Achebe, Chinua. *Morning Yet on Creation Day*. London: Heinemann, 1970.

– – –. *No Longer at Ease*. London: Heinemann, 1960.

– – –. *The Trouble with Nigeria*. Enugu: Fourth Dimension, 1983.

Asouzu, Innocent. *The Method and Principles of Complementary Reflection: In and Beyond African Philosophy*. Calabar: University Press, 2004.

Ce, Chin. 'Bards and Tyrants: Literature, Leadership and Citizenship Issues of Modern Nigeria' *Africa Literary Journal* (*ALJ*) B5, IRCALC, 2005. 3-24.

– – –. *Gamji College*. Enugu: Handel, 2002.

Davidson, Basil. *The Black Man's Burden: Africa and the Curse of the Nation State*. Ibadan: Spectrum, 1993.

Deloria, Vine Jnr. *We Talk, You Listen: New Tribes New Turf*. New York: Macmillan, 1970.

Emenyonu, Ernest. Ed. *Goatskin bags and Wisdom: New Critical Perspectives on African Literature*. Asmara: African World Press, 2000.

Fanon, Frantz. *The Wretched of the Earth*. Middlesex: Penguin, 1967.

Hamilton, Grant. "Beyond Subjectificatory Structures: Chin Ce 'In the season of Another Life'". *Journal of African Literature and Culture* (JALC) No. 3 IRCALC, 2006. 95-117.

Kekewich, Lucille Margaret "Introduction" *The Prince* Machiavelli.

Hertfordshire: Wordsworth, 1997.

Lindfors, Bernth. *African Textualities*. Asmara: Africa World Press, 1997.

Oguzie, B. E. C. "Society in Chukwuemeka Ike's Fiction: A Focus on The Potter's Wheel and Expo '77" *Goatskin Bags and Wisdom: New Critical Perspectives on African Literature*. Emenyonu, E. N. (Ed.) Asmara: Africa World Press, 2000.

Ogungbesan, Kolawole. *New West African Literature*. London: Heinemann, 1979.

Onwubiko, K. B. C. *History of West Africa Book II 1800-Present Day*. Onitsha: Africana Educational 1973

Rodney, Walter. *How Europe Underdeveloped Africa*. London: Bogle-l'Ouverture, 1972.

Soyinka, Wole. *The Man Died.* Middlesex: Penguin, 1975.

Watt, Stephen "Introduction" *The Republic*. Plato. Hertfordshire: Wordsworth, 1997.

Weiss, Bettina. Ed. *The End of Unheard Narratives: Contemporary Perspectives on South African Literature*. Heidelberg: Kalliope, 2004.

6

Pedagogy of Disillusionment

FERDINAND OYONO'S *THE OLD MAN AND THE MEDAL* AND CHIN
CE'S *GAMJI COLLEGE*

Kenneth Usongo

*F*erdinand Oyono's *The Old Man and the Medal* and Chin Ce's
Gamji College respectively constitute an indictment on colonial
French and local African leaders for the economic, political, and
social exploitation of the people of Africa. Both cases bequeath the
culture of corruption and violence instituted and entrenched in
colonial and post colonial administrations.

In *The Old Man and the Medal*, Meka, as a result of the medal
that is offered to him by the Chief of the whites, is led to believe in the
virtues of equality and brotherhood propagated by the colonizers.
However, Meka's horrendous experience with the police chief,
Gullet, awakens black consciousness regarding white hypocrisy.
More than ever before, the blacks decry their marginalization by their
oppressors and enkindle a revolutionary flame that shall arrest some
of the abuses. In *Gamji College*, through the trajectory of Tai and
Jerry, we relive the tale of moral paucity that is characteristic of an
independent African nation as the masses struggle to install some
sanctity in the conduct of public affairs.

WHITE ON BLACK / BLACK ON BLACK

The interaction between blacks/whites and blacks/blacks has been a familiar theme in most African writing, especially the novels dealing with the (post)colonial periods. While novelists like Chinua Achebe, Cyprian Ekwensi, Kenjo Jumbam and others have addressed this concern by generally indicating how blacks have often been outpaced by the dispensation proffered by the white world, Wole Soyinka and Ngugi wa Thiongo'o articulate instances of a matching resistance to Western influence. Ferdinand Oyono appears to tread the middle ground in this Africa-Europe confrontation. His submission shows an oppressed people that initially are naïve, but ultimately become aware of the tertiary role that is imposed on them by their oppressors. This is particularly the case of the villages of Doum and Zourian in *The Old Man and the Medal.* Meka, a veritable upshot of these twin villages, is subjected to harrowing series of exploitation, hypocrisy and injustice by the French. It is through his lenses that we view the lot of the oppressed black community.

On his part, the works of Chin Ce expose society and citizens who are disgusted with the conduct of black governments in a post colonial era. *Gamji College*, his second work of fiction, is illustrative of a nation that is putrid to the core as it rides on the crest of corruption. The final dissolution of its trumped-up presidential election insinuates a flicker of hope that Gamji may emerge from its inglorious past as a rejuvenated and democratic entity that can jettison suicidal and greedy politics.

Informed by Paolo Freire, Liam Kane insists that committed art is the weapon of the 'oppressed' in a world run by 'oppressors' in the hope that their education can awaken them to the injustices inflicted on them by their oppressors (12). Therefore while Ferdinand Oyono's *The Old Man and the Medal*, working within the confines of post colonial criticism, may help us reappraise Europe's biased consideration of Africa as degenerate and totally needy of redemptive Western values, with Chin Ce's *Gamji College* we come to the understanding that Africa is not a show case of impeccable values as its body politic is ridden by vices that require urgent surgery. A meaningful, ideological alternative therefore is one that can synthesize the virtues of both camps and, at the same time, shun their predatory drives. Put simply, we are inferring a post-modern philosophy that promotes a society where no one is most important and no one is least important; a society where the minority is as equally important and relevant as the majority (Iwuchukwu 386).

The Old Man retraces the bitter experiences of Meka and his kindred, on the one hand, and the travails of Gamji's students, on the other. It postulates that even though they are under the burden of (post)colonial administrations, they are eventually aware of the wars of discrimination and exploitation on them by their oppressors. In pursuing this line of action, the (post)colonial overlord disengages himself from the warning that we must be guided by a vision of the person untainted by ideological and cultural prejudices or by political and economic interests which can instill hatred and violence (Benedict 4). We revisit the tedious path to enlightenment for these downtrodden people and indicate that, following their disillusionment, things will hardly be the same as when they had warmly embraced their leadership and, in the process, wallowed in various expectations.

EXPECTATION

When Meka (*The Old Man*) receives a summons from the Commandant, he loses his peace of mind as he is struck by insomnia. He is overwhelmingly anxious about what good fortune is appended to this strong invitation in the same way that the youthful Tai (*Gamji*) braces himself for academic and moral edification at Gamji College. The elderly Meka is, therefore, obliged to wake up his snoring wife,

Kelara, to share in his excitement and he wonders how a woman, faced with the summoning of her husband before the white officer, can still enjoy the luxury of sleep: "Kelara! he roared, thumping her back. How can you sleep when your husband has troubles?" (3). At this bewildering moment, poor Meka, like Ngugi's Muthoni, can only resort to prayers as he implores God to protect him. He fails to fathom the modus operandi of French colonialism which was/is a thoroughgoing, comprehensive and deliberate penetration of a local or 'residentiary' system by the agents of an external system, who aim to restructure the patterns of organization, resource use, circulation and outlook so as to bring these into a linked relationship with their own system (Brookfield 1-2).

Following this important call, Meka dresses smartly to impress the white man. After all, among the Fong of Cameroon, the name Meka signifies loyalty and submission, especially to colonial authority. He is compelled to wear his cockroach-infested jacket, which has been hanging on the wall for ages, as a mark of respect for the Commandant. His attire, coupled with the ancient helmet above his head, is truly exotic and, in the rollicking words of Kelara, he is "like an American missionary" (4). In line with subjectifying blacks to French administration, the white priest makes Meka believe that in surrendering his land to the church, he is fulfilling a divine wish that will earn him celestial joy. As a result, Meka is seen as a model Christian, one that will shudder from a taste of the local brew, arki, for fear of not only risking imprisonment, but guilt of committing mortal sin. Notice this subterfuge of the French that is reminiscent of the age-old anecdote of the colonization of Africa that the natives were cajoled into praying to God while the white colonizer tactfully dispossessed them of their land. In concomitance was the charade of Christianity as the new converts were reminded to love and obey their foes irrespective of the situation. By isolating Meka for distinction, the French oppressors favour selected leaders rather than promoting the community as a whole. The latter course, by preserving a state of alienation, hinders the emergence of consciousness and critical intervention in a total reality (Freire 143).

The scoop is the forthcoming decoration of Meka on the 14th of July by the great Chief of all the white men in Timba. Paradoxically, the French liberation festivities are intended to hoodwink the natives that they and the French are indivisible in the quest for liberty, fraternity and equality regardless of colour and/or race. There is ululation by the women following these tidings and men strive to identify themselves with the 'heroic' Meka. By evening, this news is embellished in the understanding that the President of France is specifically coming to Doum to decorate Meka. A certain eerie feeling envelops the imminent medalist in the light of these premature celebrations: "With these white men you never know" (17).

As Meka reluctantly drives away the festive women lest they usher some misfortune for him, he is convinced that his medal is hidden in a drawer in the Commandant's desk or in the keeping of the Chief of whites in Timba. Between this day and the 14th of July, he is restless; he is fearful that he may die as he awaits his medal. His worry is greatly compounded by his inability to determine his age. Being the first person called from among several blacks cued in front of the Commandant's office, Meka considers himself a seer among blind men and a crowing cock in the midst of hens. In the pompous words of the white Officer, Meka is distinguishable because

> You have done much to forward the work of France in this country. You have given your lands to the missionaries, you have given your two sons in the war when they found a glorious death. (He wiped away an imaginary tear). You are a friend... The medal that we are going to give you means you are more than our friend. (19)

117

Meka, then, sees himself wrestling with the wind in the quest for ultimate recognition. But Ignatius Obebé thinks differently; he views the medal as trivial and a hoax, and wishes that Meka wins a more rewarding medal that is void of colonial trappings, perhaps one of salvation.

Similarly, in *Gamji College*, the college of Gamji has for some time been the pride of the natives as many youths had identified hope in this citadel of knowledge. Unfortunately, this institution has been steadily declining as marked by the political change from military autocracy to civilian democracy:

> In three years of democratic *laissez faire*, when chief executives of federal, state and local governments -not to talk of college high lords gave vent their plundering mania, everything in town, not excluding the landscape, had become a ghost of its former self. (5)

From stinking hostels to the stench reeking in the drainage system, this college remains a blemish to academia to the extent that those who enroll there are considered inmates of filth. The likes of James and Peter attempt to enkindle some veneer of hope in freshmen. These two entreat Tai to attend a fellowship crusade on campus that will, they claim, be crowned with miracles.

Attempting to mollify Tai, James stresses that all human beings are one in the eyes of God and that they are all reflections of the divine image. In Gamji, politics and religion constitute a curious blend hence the Rector's participation in the divine service. What is probably overlooked is the fact that the Rector is a nephew to His Excellency and that the marriage between politics and religion serves the goals of the politicians in deceiving and exploiting the poor. As the Squealer that he is, James warns Tai to guard against hypocritical and deceptive occult groups parading the university premises. The only safe fellowship is that of Gamji College that can contend the

118

seductions of 'nefarious' cults sprouting on the campus. In other words, only the ruling regime can adequately satisfy the concerns of the majority; any opposition party should not be tolerated because it is myopic and diabolical. But very soon, this sweeping assertion, like Meka's bloated medal, will begin to dissipate.

FRAGMENTATION

Oyono shows that the various festivities organized in Meka's house on the eve of the medal award are at variance with local expectations. His compound bustles with animation and pride and poor Meka is compelled to stitch a special 'zazou' jacket, purchase shoes for the occasion. While his shoes greatly pain him, he apparently does not have an option if he has to appear decent before the white man. He is a determined man as evident in the clenching of his teeth in a bid to put on leather shoes. He finds it extremely difficult to walk and this is a subtle reminder of the friendship purported by the whites towards him and his compatriots.

Meka's increasing sleeplessness visibly portends the falsehood enshrined in the medal. He is anxious about its colour and size, but is consoled that it may not be a replica of a catechist's medallion nor resemble the inconsequential one won by Ignatius Obebé. It is only in this distinction in enormity that his fame shall rise, making him the envy of Doum and beyond. He overreaches himself when he imagines clasping the white man in a warm embrace and offering him a basket of eggs. His exuberance as the medal is pinned on his chest places him, in this appreciation of Ngugi wa Thiongo'o, as "an ugly savage screaming with gleaming white teeth and looking at the reassuring presence of his white master" (Heywood 6).

Regrettably, Meka is confounded to observe that while he stands alone in a painted circle under an excruciatingly hot sun, the whites take shelter in the shade of Father Vandermayer's veranda. The black

119

recipient is abandoned to himself for unending hours, deprived of the warmth of his fellow Africans that are several feet away from him. He notices that not only is Pipiniaki's medal different from his, but the white merchant receives a reassuring embrace as the medal is carefully placed on his chest: "Then Meka saw the great Chief grasp his shoulder and put his cheeks one after the other against the cheeks of the Greek" (92).

When it is his turn, his medal is not only inferior in quality, but in place of an embrace, he gets a handshake from the Chief of the whites. The latter finds it condescending to rub his body against the sweaty bosom of Meka. A keen observer in the crowd aptly comments about the triviality of the medal in compensation for the great sacrifice of Meka towards the French cause: "I think they ought to have covered him in medals. That would have been a bit more like it. To think he lost his land and his sons just for that…" (94)

This remark sends Kelara weeping profusely. It now dawns on her and her female folk that Meka had traded too much for too little; and that the medal is largely disproportionate to the two sons lost in a war. It is an antique as proven when Meka taps the holy Vandermayer to determine the lieu of the reception party; he is ignored by the white priest. This is a vivid illustration that the medal alone cannot break the social barriers between the blacks and the whites, and that the latter are hesitant to welcome attempts by the former to fully fraternize with them. Put differently, the acclaimed friendship is a veneer that cannot penetrate the skin colour.

Acting partly under the influence of wine, the blacks gulp down glasses of whisky to the disenchantment of the whites. In the words of Meka, "If you want to know what your friend thinks of you, drink a few glasses with him" (106). Armed with this conviction, he challenges the whites on the notion of brotherhood by inviting them for dinner at his compound. The High Commissioner politely turns down this offer intimating that because of his busy schedule, he can only partake of Meka's goat in spirit. Ironically, he feasts with the white medalist. His rebuff of Meka clearly underscores French hypocrisy and crystallizes black criticism of the love and friendship encapsulated in the medal. They are soon vindicated in that when the mood becomes festive in the Community Centre, the whites find this embarrassing and abandon the blacks to themselves. No sooner do they celebrate their newly found freedom than Gullet and his men order them to quit the hall. They are now considered scallywags. Bit by bit, it dawns on the blacks that they had blown out of proportion the significance of the medal; they analysed it literally against the metaphorical exegesis of the French.

We can compare this treatment meted to the underdogs to that of the Nigerian story of Chin Ce where draped in a green and white agbada, reminiscent of the national colours of Nigeria, President Baba Sonja, the Kadiye of the land, cuts a grotesque image before his younger national Tai: "The diseased-looking pot-bellied old man had never inspired him for once as a president" 18). After pouring several diatribes on youths for being injurious to the nation, this mischievous politician implores everybody to support him as he draws a fallacious link between him and God: "I call on everyone to support the vision of our country as directed by God" (18). Earlier on, the Parliament had exposed his chicanery by rejecting a proposed Bill that put God in the centre-spread of the national map. In these inflated words of the President lies the post colonial drive to dupe the nation and subvert the people's aspirations:

> Arise Compatriots
> God's holy call obey
> To serve the Lord thy God
> With ho-liness and faith
> The labours of the saints ago

121

Shall no more be in vain
To serve the lord thy God
One na-tion bound in justice
Peace and Unity (19).

The stress in the words "ho--liness" and "na--tion" accentuates the falsehood of the politician in establishing a harmonious link between these two streams. Baba presents himself as an enlightened despot in that as God's representative on earth, he cherishes the welfare of the nation, especially the youths. The political pretence is unmistakable as we notice the sycophantic Dr Jeze describe the presidential 'speech' as the "Gamji declaration" (19). The President and his cronies ensure that the masses are brainwashed as the latter intone a new national anthem that extols the virtues of politics and religion. Rimi Merenge, the Head of State's alter ego, spares no effort in hailing the new leadership of Baba and imprecating youths for breeding the culture of skepticism, particularly within a college milieu. Leader Obu, the Pastor's partner in this hoax, reiterates the sinfulness of youths as he supplicates God to cleanse them of the vice of mistrust. The service culminates in the religious pranks of some fellowship members as they fling themselves to the ground in a spiritual frenzy intended to underscore the overriding power of prayers. Like the case of Oyono's story, religion is used by the administration to maintain a stronghold on the population.

As the President's acolytes –James and Peter– insist that Baba Sonja is a born again Christian and, therefore, an instrument of the Lord. Tai, like Soyinka's Igwezu, retorts that Baba is to blame for the collapse of the nation. Confronted by Tai's intransigence to attend campus service, the insidious duo intimate that he has lately joined a cult or, connotatively, aligned with an opposition party.

In the second section of the story, Churchill decries the plight of the masses by situating them as victims of "Arrest and Detention. Advance and Deviance" (59). The citizens are perpetually subjected to various abuses orchestrated by their inept ruling governments. It may be posited that the youths in Gamji take alcohol as opium, a ruse by the despicable regime to deaden their consciences in the wake of state atrocities. As earlier stated, while the French ban the consumption of liquor in Doum and Zourian ostensibly to encourage the purchase of foreign brands, the Gamji government allows its subjects to drench in it for the purpose of docility.

As Churchill himself tells us, Gamji's rulers are, therefore, a reflection of petty tyrants across Africa that continuously harp on patriotism and sacrifice on the part of the oppressed citizenry as these leaders loot and plunder the economy, and stifle any opposition:

> And he made a few flattering noises about sacrifice and patriotism from his country men, except of course some public enemies and politicians he had clamped in jai. (61)

Like most of the new nations born out of the ashes of colonialism, Gamji is a travesty of democracy and freedom. Such post colonial states resonate with various negations, says Churchill: "Everything that Machiavelli thought was possible in a Hobbessian state, those scumbags epitomized them all in the black man" (62). Their newfangled Presidents always abandon the object and chase the shadow. Churchill succinctly captures this aberration in this remark: "Some fools started War against Indiscipline when it should have read War against Injustice" [1] (62).

DISILLUSIONMENT

Be it in the case of Oyono's world or Ce's Gamji state, the masses successfully unveil the cloak of oppression and fathom the deception that has been progressively practised on them by (post)colonial authorities. Their experiences with the callous administration awaken their consciousness to the necessity to arrest the dehumanizing treatment to which they are being subjected. How and to what extent both communities succeed in severing ties with the agents of evil will be appraised in the following paragraphs.

As the blacks in Oyono's *The Old Man* scramble out of the Community Centre, Meka, dead drunk, is abandoned to himself in the collapsing building that is being buffeted by heavy rain and a violent storm. It is as if nature and the French are partners in this torture. He painfully wriggles himself out of the wreckage of the hall and is comforted that his Christian medal, Saint Christopher, is tenaciously clinging to his chest. However, the one given to him by the Chief of the whites is detached from his coat. Is this to remind him that the medal is simply a gimmick by the whites to cajole him into believing in their friendship, a loud-sounding nothing devoid of substance? He is soon apprehended by Gullet's men and manhandled as a criminal, a prowler in the European quarter. He is dragged in muddy water like an old sack, kicked in his back, and insulted by a constable in spite of the fact that he identifies himself as the recipient of a French medal. Symbolically, Meka's loss of the medal is a subtle reminder to the blacks that, with minimum effort, they can shake off the colonial caste.

He is incarcerated on the flimsy charge of: "Loitering with suspicious intent... No lights, No papers... nothing..." (126). Like Ellison's invisible man, Meka and his peers have lost their identity within their fatherland, outlived their usefulness, and are enjoined to redefine their relevance to the white cause now that the latter wields the rein of power in the native land. In fact, Meka is now fit for the toilet or grave as the constables express their worry that in detaining him, he may taint the freshly painted walls of the cell. The inability of the constables to spell Laurence, Meka's Christian name which they write as Roro, supremely attests that he is a nonentity in the white administered Doum. It is while he is in detention that he is conscientized that he and his comrades had been systematically humiliated and pilfered by the colonial authorities. The mournful cry of the night bird is symbolic of their plight in the hands of a monstrous administration.

Early the next morning, the handcuffed Meka is brought before Gullet. The latter manifests his contempt for him by spitting in his face. As if in complete disillusionment, Meka responds to the question on his identity asked by Gullet thus: "I am a very great fool, who yesterday still believed in the white man's friendship" (135). Probably embarrassed by these words, Gullet slots a cigarette into Meka's mouth in an attempt to soothe the latter. This type of violence on the part of the oppressors prevents the oppressed from being fully human (Freire, 1970:44). Meka's calm in the face of this provocation underlines his friendly temperament. He seems to either subscribe to Ghandist non-violence or adhere greatly to Blakian love in place of hate as evident in 'The little Black Child' where a black child professes love to a white child, not by precept, but by example: "And then I'll stand and strike his silver hair, / And be like him, and he will then love me" (Hunt 740).

Gullet's dismissive words to Meka constitute an innuendo as he informs the latter that he shall be given another medal and that he should always come along with a lamp to town. This utterance again situates Meka as one without an identity, one that is reminded to always sacrifice for the whites to notice his presence. The 'invisible' Meka is instructed to demonstrate his visibility through permanent support of French interest. This time, he is undeceived by French hypocrisy. His experience with Gullet remains deeply ingrained in his mind as thereafter it dawns on him that he was wooing a leopard. His disillusionment is total as inscribed in his words to a passer-by: "The whites...just the whites..." (140).

This realization ably represents his edification from his interaction with them; they remain chameleons and the beholder is perpetually challenged to identify their colour at each appearance. His closing words in the novel: "I'm just an old man now..." (167) reiterate the point that he has learnt an unpalatable lesson from the medal. The whites largely succeed in subduing the blacks because of the latter's generally submissive and receptive attitude. They eternalize the vice of neocolonialism which, to Kwame Nkrumah, is imperialism in its final and perhaps its most dangerous form. The essence is that the State which is subject to it is, in theory, independent and has all the outward trappings of international sovereignty. In reality, its economic system and thus its political policy are directed from outside (Smith 1999-208).

Likewise in Chin Ce's representation of postcolonial Nigeria, the feeling of despair in Gamji is amply registered in the observations of Milord, Dogo and Femi. Milord is so disgusted with the opulence of evil in Gamji to the extent that he sees Bisi as a microcosm of these vices. Lacking in natural beauty, she is deeply meretricious, a symbol of the drifting freedom and democracy that the people are yearning for. The new nation is a shadow of itself as attested by the frequent power outages. The frustrations of the youths are reflected in the tramp lifestyles of Milord, Dogo and Femi with the one sleeping on the floor, the others puking from the window and toilet. It is as if they are venting their disappointment at the much acclaimed independence.

There is further discontentment in Gamji as evident in the short listing of five 'mad' men to run for the presidency. Napoleon, a belated contestant in the sixth position, is yet to buy the first round of drinks synonymous with the routine corruption characteristic of most presidential elections in Africa. We are definitely irked upon learning that his singular leadership trait is a predilection for cigarette brands:

> He was wont to display the packets in long rows on his bookshelf.
> His sense of neat arrangement was impeccable when it came to
> empty cigarette packs, empty boxes of matches and used up
> lighters. (81)

To exacerbate an already ugly scenario, he is notorious for violating orders, taunting women on their buttocks and wearing dark glasses at night. Deceptively professing neutrality, Napoleon opines a de facto law of most African presidential elections, especially the situation of incumbents: "No politician ever contemplates failure in this business" (82). As an afterthought, he affirms that if elections were to bar him from the State house, the pistol will smoothen his way. His modus operandi remains that "All problems, and their cures are at the tip of his fingers!" (86). Like most incipient tyrants, Napoleon declares that his race for the presidency is an attempt to rescue the masses from the dictatorship of the bourgeoisie. The audience is, of course, bored to listen to his balderdash, one that is in the tradition of Dickens' Sleary. Napoleon, like his five rivals, pours out the same mumbo-jumbo to the electorate. None is any different from the other in mediocrity.

Chin Ce reveals how Gamji is evidently torn apart by the rival candidates clamouring for the presidency. These political crooks are largely identified along ethnic colorations (dominant/dominated, majority/minority, dark/fair etc) and not following credible, ideological positions geared at improving the welfare of the masses. The cumulative effect is the polarization of the nation along cardinal points-North/South, West/East. It is true to say that many [Gamjians] today see the state from the prism of their ethnic groups and the status, access and opportunities that accrue to them (Osaghae 55). Ipso facto, the other five presidential candidates consolidate their bids by

127

subverting the candidature of Napoleon on grounds of non-alignment. In other words, he has not sufficiently anchored himself within a specific ethnicity.

Following the above trend of demonization, it is not surprising that the political campaign degenerates into a mayhem. In the ensuing altercation a presidential candidate Ege –one who arguably rose above ethnic partisanship– is slain. Curiously, Ce's blend of native names (Ege) with foreign ones (Napoleon) allegorically represents the tussle for supremacy between local and foreign ideologies, between African assumptions and European ethics in Gamji.

Ultimately, the outcome of the election is a burlesque of justice. It is flawed by rigging and intimidation in the hope of making an indigenous candidate victorious: "Blood will flow... We will teach these strangers a lesson!" (112). Regrettably, Gamji College Fellowship negates its role as the watchdog of equity and fair play by instructing people to vote for M because of his so called divinity. The sick looking registrar that oversees the elections is symptomatic of an electoral system in dire need of reform. Jerry is discontented by the entire election procedure as he wonders aloud how many souls still have to be sacrificed so that Gamji becomes a civilized society. He quits the electoral commission convinced that the whole exercise is an insult to justice.

Predictably, the election is halted by violence that sweeps across Gamji. This new nation is in desperate need of definition following the contours of justice, freedom and democracy. It is not any better than Oyono's world. Both societies are crippled by the vices of colonialism and post colonialism, dependence and independence; the quest for a consummate nationhood that fuses the genuine aspirations of the oppressed masses remains disturbingly elusive for Gamji.

Oyono structurally splits his novel into three parts corresponding to the expectations, broken dreams, and disillusionment of Meka as each section of the story tackles these triple phases of the hero's life in the process of pedagogy. It also mirrors the extended patience of the blacks against protracted French provocation. This sophisticated division seems to affirm the discrepancy between the promises of the French and their fulfillment. And that their word constitutes a veritable tossed yo-yo that clearly leaves aspirants frustrated. Indeed, Meka suffers from self deception as he earlier had confidence in the French; his final delusion by them is revealing as he and his brethren are tutored that in dinning with the French, they need a ladle in scooping the bowl. In other words, his experience constitutes a ringing challenge to his counterparts that they should be wary as they flirt with a hyena. Now, they have been sufficiently conscientized that the struggle for their rights must be initiated and sustained by them; it does not depend on the benevolence of the colonial master. They had been overtaken by their naivety and ignorance into believing that the medal was a magic wand to their problems. Far from it; the good is yet to come through their commitment in liberating themselves from the claws of oppression and its attendant vices.

Chin Ce's *Gamji College*, aside its graphic illustrations depicting the shifting moods of the story, is also skillfully divided into three crucial phases, namely, "The Cross", "The Bottle", and "The Gun" respectively representing the intoxicating influence of the bible on the mindset; the liberating force of alcohol on people as they reveal their innermost minds; and the resultant violence and chaos unleashed by the gun –white man's legacy of brigandage in Africa. This meticulous structure reflects a floating society in need of justice, stability and peace; Gamji is miniature Africa grappling with the throes of independence as some of the injustices of colonialism are replayed.

While in Ferdinand Oyono's novel there is cautious optimism that Meka and his comrades can successfully break the chains of oppression and possibly get embroiled in the vicious cycle of anomaly typical of post colonial Gamji, Chin Ce's heroes seemingly do not present the same degree of commitment to stem the tide of violence. However, a common denominator between the people of both fictions is the self hallucination that leads to disillusionment triggered by (post)colonial forces. Despondent as the future may look for Gamji, a revolutionary flame is ignited in Tai and Jerry as both vituperate the ills of the new nation. The 'beautyful ones' are in the process of being born. They are seen as harbingers to a more embracing, political dispensation that may eschew the abuses and excesses of the preceding age. Gamji, Doum and Zourian will make ideal nations when they effectively harness solid Western principles of good governance and freedom alongside African values of brotherhood and communalism, or when they adroitly lubricate Western steel with African grease.

NOTES

[1]The slogan of "War against Indiscipline" was en vogue during the military regime of President Buhari of Nigeria. Enforced by his 'No. 2 strongman', Tunde Idiabon, it restored some civic discipline among the ordinary citizens while, paradoxically, senior government officials shamelessly pillaged the nation's economy.

WORKS CITED

Adults Learning. Vol.17, Issue 2.Oct. 2005,

Benedict XVI. 'Message to Celebrate World Day of Peace', 1 Jan. 2007.

Brookfield, H.C. *Colonialism, Development and Independence: The Case of the Melanesian Islands in the South Pacific*. Cambridge: Cambridge UP.1972.

Ce, Chin. *Gamji College*. Enugu: Handel Books.2002.

Freire, Paolo. *Pedagogy of the Oppressed*. New York: Continuum. 1970.

Iwuchukwu, Marinus Chijoke. "Democracy in a Multireligious and Cultural Setting." *Journal of General Evolution,* 2003, Vol.59, Issue 5, pp. 381-390.

Heywood, Christopher ed. *Perspectives on African Literature*. London: Heinemann.1971.

Hunt, Douglas ed. *The Riverside Anthology of Literature*. Boston: Houghton Mifflin Company.1988.

Mendo Ze, Gervais. *La prose Romanesque de Ferdinand Oyono*. Paris: Groupe Media International.1984.

Nfah-Abbenyi, Juliana Makuchi. *Gender in African Women's Writing*. Bloomington: Indiana UP.1997.

Osaghae, Eghosa. "Explaining the Changing Patterns of Ethnic Politics in Nigeria." *Nationalism & Ethnic Politics*, Autumn 2003, Vol. 9, Issue 3, pp. 54-73.

Oyono, Ferdinand. *The Old Man and the Medal*. London: Heinemann. 1967.

Peck, John and Martin Coyle. *Literary Terms and Criticism*. New York: Palgrave.2002.

Smith, T ed. *The End of the European Empire: Decolonization after World War II*. Lexington: D.C. Heath.1975.

Sung, Kim II. *On Revolutionary Literature and Arts*. London: Africa Ltd.1972.

7

Locating the Voice

THE POST-MODERNIST NARRATIVE MAZE OF *THE VISITOR*

Okuyade Ogaga

LITERARY MODERNISM AND THE AFRICAN NOVEL

The publication of Ayi Kwei Armah's novel *The Beautyful Ones Are Not Yet Born* may have marked the entrance of modernist tradition in African artistic canvas. Chinua Achebe whose debut novel *Things Fall Apart* published ten years earlier before Armah's, occupies an inaugural and canonical position in the history and evolution of the African novel, was unsatisfied with Armah's experimentation and had observed that the book is "sick, not with the sickness of Ghana, but with sickness of the human condition" (26). Regardless of numerous African texts with modernist permutations, critics have been reticent about this aspect of the African novel. African writers explore the consciousness of modernism which foregrounds the sense of despair, disorder and anarchy, as perfect medium for them to conveying on the one hand their nostalgia for the past, with its imperfections and limitation, and on the other hand their galling ironic indictment of the present. From this dimension, Bradbury and Macfarlan's definition of modernism become relevant as they describe modernism as "the movement towards sophistication and mannerism, towards introspection, technical display and internal self-skepticism" (26). The above description of the concept shows that as a medium of experimentation modernism does not simply suggest the presence of sophistication, difficulty and novelty as the description above connotes. It also suggests bleakness, darkness, alienation and disintegration the modernist artist invariably becomes an artist under a specific historical strain. It becomes glaring that for the African novelist, colonialism and post-colonialism are the strain that launched him/her into the international literary scene.

Modernism flowered into artistic fruition from the West during the first quarter of the twentieth century. The twentieth century was a century of extremes which ushered in a new world order that became shocking and frightening to humanity. Virginia Woolf, a modernist in her own right, was prompted to remark that "on or about December 1910 human nature changed" (qtd. in Hewit (1). Through her hyperbolic assertion, Virginia Woolf meant to suggest that there is a frightening dislocation between the traditional and the chaotic present and that the line of history has faulted, perhaps broken, and humans now assume a parenthetical existence it became difficult to define man in clear terms (this part is not that clear...). Modernist literature suggests that human nature indeed changed, and probably a few decades before the date given by Woolf. At the dawn of the twentieth century, the world recorded a barrage of cataclysmic developments, which sent it reeling from its fragile idyllic balance. Since Literature heavily relies on society for its expression, a review of the historical events that characterized the twentieth century will no doubt explicate the reasons for the emergence of modernism. Of all the events that characterized the twentieth century, the two World Wars remain the most devastating and major accelerators of the history of mankind.

Alan Munton defines modernism as "a radical dissatisfaction with the commonsense view of the real" (2). This radical dissatisfaction is what informs Friedman's description of the structure of the modernist novel as gradually changing "from the structure of a ladder to the structure of a cobweb"(415). Friedman further claims that "the energy of the novel shifted from a polar distribution between its centres –the individual self and the social world – to an unbalanced concentration of the self" (416). And David Jones describes modernist novels as the literature of "nowness" (109). Considering the cataclysmic upheavals and the anarchical ambience that revolutionized the novel at the dawn of the twentieth century and the general breakdown in agreement about continuity and order in society, Jose Ortega dubs the modernist construct as "the dehumanization of art" (213). Modernism hinges heavily on radical innovation and experimentation. Herein lies its complexity.

African literature is encapsulated in world literature; it does not exist in isolation or stand on its own. Like other Western writers who artistically documented the terrifying developments of their world, so has colonialism and the post-independence conditions of Africa become the apocalyptic moments that have spurred African writers –especially novelists labeled within the second phase of the evolutionary process of the African novel. In Charles Nnolim's contention, the Nigerian "(post) modernist trend may have developed independently of Europe's influence and might have come about both from the use of fantasy and exaggerations we find as the staple elements of our folklore…" (64) Nnolim even goes further to identify Amos Tutuola as one of its major precursors in Nigeria.

The general discontent with colonial rule led to the struggle for the demand for independence or self-rule. The hope and anticipation for independence was interpreted as the panacea for the many years of colonial subjugation and brutality. However, after independence had come to most African states it became obvious that this was not the route to indigeneous bliss. What Africa needed most was socio-economic emancipation which the leaders were been unable to provide for the masses of the continent. Coupled with this harsh reality are the neo-colonial tendencies of emergent African rulership.

The dire economic hardship and the political instability that characterize many African post-colonial nations expose more than before the intolerable gap between the rich and the poor and the permeating corruption. Precisely because of the politics and social afflictions that tend to characterize numerous African countries, many writers of the continent are often classified as engaged writers, as instruments of change whose job is to expose, in one way or another, the evils of society. As Tanure Ojaide puts it: "a certain notion had begun to gain ground among young writers and critics that ...African writers have to be an instrument of change", especially "in periods when the generality of the populace had become economically and politically marginalized" (6). Similarly, Chin Ce himself opines that the new generation of African writers, poets in particular, have "become the chronicler of yester pillage by modern political brigands, or the recorder of the pitiful howling of fallen roofs" (Emezue ARI).

CHIN CE'S POST-MODERNIST NARRATIVE

Without necessarily having to label Chin Ce a modernist, it is clear that *The Visitor* possesses narrative techniques that are very much in agreement with those used by modernist literature in general. Chin Ce can be situated within the third generation of Nigerian novelists who may have contributed to a renewed efflorescence of the novel in Nigeria. Throughout his oeuvres, Ce mediates on various aspects of the human condition: love, solitude, pain, death, faith. In treating these themes, he moves seamlessly between philosophical reflection and the description of intimate details of everyday life. His lyrical voice continues to foreground the underpinning of his art; his ability to continually explore new literary forms and his passionate and earnest personal vision create an ambience that is spiritual without being sentimental.

Although the thrust of this discourse concentrates on the discussion of the narrative strategies employed by Ce in *The Visitor*, it is imperative to enumerate some modernist narrative devices. Modernism exhibits a miscellany of narrative experiments and innovations such as multiple voices and viewpoint, stream of consciousness, the disruptions of logical or temporal sequence, juxtapositions, repetitions, elaborate speculations on the powers and limits of language (meta-narrative and meta-linguistic concerns) and sophisticated rhetorical complexities.

Structurally modern fiction hardly emphasizes logical arrangement, since the world which it seeks to reflect lacks any logical or stable meaning. The formlessness of the modernist novel is consequently a reflection of the writer's vision of the world. There is an emphasis on literary experimentation and each writer is expected to explore and adopt whichever techniques he/she feels best express and convey his/her thoughts and state of mind. Thematically, modern fiction is concerned with problems of isolation, frustration and hopelessness. It also questions the existence of evil in man and the futility of human life. Moreover, modernist fiction displays less interest in character portrayal. What matters is the individual in relation to the world: characters can no longer be assumed, as in the past, to be fixed and synthetic entities with a set of traits available through notations of conduct and report of psychic condition. There is a shift from type to individual characters: the personas that we encounter in the modernist novel do fit a set type, throwing us out of the familiar terrain of facile reconnaissance.

Being paradigmatic of the modernist novel, *The Visitor* also displays a fissured character portrayal: characters are not regarded as coherent and easily definable entities. Character portrayal becomes a complicated affair, a sort of psychic battlefield, an insoluble puzzle or the occasion for a flow of perception and sensations. Modernists seek to explore ideas which perplex their mind in the process of attempting to understand their world. Novels are characterized by an achronological ordering of events: events are scattered and seemingly unconnected, yet they are fused together in their own unique way. Such events are presented are like different pictures, which reflect the different states of mind of people in the society.

At first glance we immediately notice the fragmenting nature of narration in *The Visitor*. As the different characters tell their stories the plot of the novel develops rapidly. However, the manner in which events and incidents are presented in the novel may leave the reader confused. For example, the novel begins in the prologue with Mensa's confession which is not recorded in the city of Aja and yet the confession seems to be preserved in Erin land. And after the prologue, in page one we meet Erie in the land Erin, battling to recall something about his identity, and especially his past. In the epilogue we meet another character, Deego, who is half awake; this character is caught between the realities of the worlds: the physical world and the 'hallucinatory' world. Yet as one reads further, it becomes obvious that these characters are the same entity –just one individual. The entire narrative is realized through memory. One realizes that one is in the midst of a bizarre psychological struggle that could turn absurd and strange for the reader because at the concluding chapter, the epilogue, Mensa and Erie dissolve into Deego's mind and thus all three become one single entity. Thus Amanda Grants notes that *The Visitor* is a story in which three dimensions of existence affecting three principal players Erie, Mensa and Deego interrelate continuously to create an unbreakable thread and posit a statement on the continuation of individual responsibility over and above mere existential needs ("Memory" 24).

Depicting post-independence Nigeria, the contemporary urban habitat of Aja is the border country between poverty, corruption and crime. The novel gives account of the physical and psychological state of the country's socio-political and economic situation on the individual citizen, thereby eloquently bringing to bear a mired nation made filthy by the economic miasma created by the depraved rulers. Thus the narrative is scattered and fragmented. Chin Ce employs the first person narrative, and the omniscient narrative techniques respectively. The beginning of the prologue is rendered from the first person point of view; however, this voice is ambivalent. It is not only anonymous, but amorphous because it is not attached to a physical entity. It becomes clear that this voice is only trapped in the wind. It is now left for the reader to trace this voice to a body or an identity. The tracing of the voice becomes the conduit through which the plot of the novel is propagated.

The second perspective is realized from the omniscient point of view. This is highlighted by the presence of the voices of Mensa, Sena, Jaci, Omo, Erie, Uzi, and Grandad. The first person narrative which is used in the epilogue complicates the omniscient viewpoint of the subsequent narrative. These narrative strategies are both triangular, and at the same time have an onion bulb shape which shall be further explained diagrammatically in the course of this discussion. The voice of Mensa which is recounted through memory, and the voices of Sena, Jaci, Erie, Uzi and Ade's are encapsulated or coated in Deego's voice, which seems to be the most tangible of all the voices. These three narrative strategies seem to form three different layers. Each layer seems to be in a world of its own yet they are organically connected by the outermost layer. Each layer when opened –especially the second account in the omniscient perspective– discloses smaller, and subtler layers than the first. As David Ker contends, "pluralization of world view is a common feature of modernism" (8). Chin Ce's novel shows a modernist obsession with pluralization and repetition. This device makes conception less exacting since the multi-voiced consciousness leads to continuous disruption in the narrative process.

The scattered wholeness of *The Visitor* is fore-grounded in the narratological devices. Charles Altieri, trying to explain the diffused connectedness of modernist art, remarks that writers of the time clearly "articulate a grammar or stylistic possibilities... in a variety of combination" (23) while Susan Lenser asserts that "point of view is the stylistic philosophic center of a novel" (60). Ce's narratology permits a diversification or miscellany of consciousness to reflect on the main concerns of his novel and this gives the reader the responsibility of putting the pieces together. Warren Beck gives a blueprint of the modernist narrative strategy:

> There is an absolute, no eternal pure white radiance in such presentation but rather the strain of many colours, refracted and shifting in kaleidoscopic suspension, about the center of man's enigmatic behaviour and fate, within the drastic orbit or mortality. (153)

In *The Visitor*, modernist tenets of both disjointedness and shifting points-of-view will no doubt stun the reader. The narrative thrives on three different narrative perspectives: the third person omniscient point of view, the "I –witness and confessant" and the "I –protagonist" points of view. These points of view are further relumed through the relaying of the thought of some of the characters like Erie, Jaci, Sena and Ade. With these three narrative perspectives employed in the novel, the story is distorted and guarantees the reader the opportunity to perceive the story from different dimensions.

Panthea Reid describes this technique as "an incremental faceting device of shifting, spreading, and filling, patterned after the artists' breaking and bending and reassembling planes on their canvasses"(101-102).

In order to accommodate his numerous narrators, Ce employs a filmic cum photographic device by which he unifies voices and thoughts. At the first narrative level the "I witness cum confessant" is used by Mensa to recount his confession:

> I am one of the staunch youths of Ironi. I have done jobs for chief, carried guns, smuggled things used to rig elections like police uniforms, ammunition, and all. I also took part in some operations at Seme border. We do our job, we get paid. Until this one, chief refused to pay me. Why? Something is there. Something that shouldn't concern him. Therefore I planned to get my money by all means ... (7)

This voice (actually an extract of Mensa's confession now moved up to the beginning prologue) is unconnected with the voices that follow immediately and seems anonymous at first reading. Coupled with its untraceable quality, the voice ends abruptly with an ellipsis. Graphologically, the search for this voice becomes the major burden of the reader. Although this voice reoccurs (170), it is still anonymous, especially because Mensa and Erie seem to be the same entity.

The second narrative technique is the 'omniscient' point of view, where the reader meets the main characters of the novel. This narrative perspective is one of the most complex because it oscillates between Aja and Erin lands. It begins right from the prologue, where we meet some young men who are smugglers in an operation, tagged 'Buff'. Mensa is a member of this gang. He hopes to get a million naira from the deal, if everything goes well. The mission was accomplished and immediately the scene switches to Erie in Erin land. From this dimension Erie seems to be the omniscient observer. The narrative switches back to Aja, where we meet Omo and Mensa warming up for an onslaught or an attack with their riotous and righteous might. From this level it becomes evident that Mensa was not given his share of the raid in the prologue.

The third narrative strategy is employed in relaying Deego's state of mind which is like a long protracted moment of awaking the surreal moment between sleep and waking up, as if in a permanent state of wakefulness, on the threshold between the conscious and the unconscious. It is the third perspective that bequeaths the garb and accoutrement of reality to the entire narrative because at a point, Deego dimly wakes up: "In the instant I was wide awake. My eyes darted furtively around the house, alert, not feeling drowsy in any degree. It took one minute to take in my surroundings again" (195). It becomes glaring that Deego was initially watching a movie which runs into his psychological networking. Chin Ce calcifies these narrative devices by moving his narrative from the linearity of the traditional plot into the psychological network of his characters thereby exposing their thoughts and intentions. This modernist technique, often tagged stream-of-consciousness narrative, relies solely on internal description and the reader must deduce external plot or action from the thoughts of the characters. Ce utilizes this narrative technique in different ways. He tends to keep the narrative within the thoughts of a particular character for a long period of time. *The Visitor* is almost completely, composed of the internal thoughts and realities of its protagonist, Mensa-Erie-Deego, only occasionally turning to the internal realities of another character.

On the other hand, Ce presents a collage of internal realities, moving rapidly from one character to the next. On other occasions, this technique functions as flash back. For example, it is through the flashback technique that the reader understands how Sena and Mensa meet the very first time in the office of the youth chair, Alhaji Ismini Jaguda. Ce also uses this means to recount Jaci's first meeting with Sena and to relay Ade's thought especially his opinion of the police force, junior officers and his superiors. This technique allows the reader to compare the widely differing versions of reality presented by the different characters. By employing such strategy, the novelist illustrates how a subjective and internal reality is more important than any sort of external or societal forces.

Most importantly, our narrator uses the stream-of-consciousness narrative to achieve an extremely detached relationship to his novel. By allowing every thought which passes through the minds of his characters, he never emphasizes which thoughts are inconsequential and which are not. Such evaluation is left for the reader to decide. Accordingly, the author's judgments or specific thoughts, ideas, and themes are often silent and not easily discernible. Ce also makes use of a new perspective: the cinematic flow and cutting from scene to scene. This technique is well explored in the incident where Mensa flees his home because of the double homicide he has committed and the scene where the vigilante corps members chase him through, until Jaci's car runs off the road. We see Mensa (150-151) incapacitated in the scene of the accident, and all of a sudden the narrative shifts to Jaci and later (155) Mensa's encounter with the Corps members reoccurs. We again encounter the same scene (170) and finally the corps members decide Mensa's fate (173). The fragmented narrative style used in *The Visitor* could be diagrammatically represented thus:

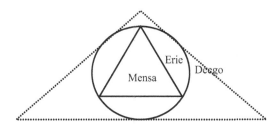

From the outside Deego bridges the gulf between the world of fantasy and the real world. Without his world the whole story will become a mere fantasy. He gives the entire story a tinge of credibility. Deego's world is not wholly tangible but surrealistic. This world is the existential borderline between *'awakeness'* and dream hence his world is dotted. Invariably the reader perceives the story from his dream 'eyes'. However, Mensa's world is the innermost world and is triangular because it is realized through memory. It is Erie's world that makes Mensa's world *mean*. Erie's world is amorphous.

At this narrative level, everything floats in the air. It is the all knowing world. From this world Ce, through Erie's eyes, foregrounds the underpinning of the material world which the inner triangle represents. The material world reflects the materialistic drive of the individuals who people the world (110-8). Everything to them is characterized by money. So that when they transcend the material to the ancestral world, the first thing that comes to their mind is money ('Naira'). From Erie's eyes the reader is once again, as in *Children of Koloko*, exposed to the folly of the rulers and the debility of the masses. From this perspective it becomes clear that the youth is an endangered group, because they are trapped between the greed and egocentricism of the politicians. They are not only instruments for orchestrating crisis but they are also victims. This assertion is substantiated in the text:

> The transaction went smoothly: arms for the boys. The boys had become the willing trigger for all political power diggers while the arms ensured the survival of all the decadent, ruling governments of the region. For Mensa, this was fair enough deal, as long as he had his cut. The politicians ruined the country directly; they, the youths only ran the errands. (9)

Further in Erin land Tuma, during the communal meeting while addressing the ancient assembly, comments: "Here again our records are incomplete... men, women in their prime of life, bombed to pieces, hanged till death, or shot by the authorities of their country..." (180). The imminent endangerment of the Nigerian youth population seems to be one of the thematic hubs in Ce's oeuvres. This concern runs through his short fiction *Children of Koloko, Gamji College* and most of his poetry collections.

In *The Visitor*, Chin Ce possesses the ability to create a work of fiction that allows for a pleasant reading experience without realizing a central plot. He chooses to explore the narrative possibilities of bringing several characters through one single day in time. Although the incidence in the novel, no doubt should span more than one day but since the entire narrative is rallied through Deego's subconscious, it could pass as an event of just a day. The novel possesses terrifying hallucinatory elements but the plot structure redeems it from mere fanciful recreation of absurdities, since the system of plot development creates the future through anticipation and the past through memory. This narrative technique works well because it mainly focuses on the 'Mensa-Erie-Deego world view', his inner workings, and his exploration and sensory experience of the world surrounding him. For example, Erie notices that Mensa, "had lifted his chin, shaking his head in the process. Something about the fellow was stirring a faint chord of familiarity, a déjà vu of sorts, in him" (13). Through the character of Erie, who is struggling to know himself beyond his new self –the present, his residual self image, Ce compels the reader to consider possibilities beyond the material world. This narrative technique moves the action forward and simultaneously delves into the life and inner workings of Erie, bringing his soul to the reader and opening up the possibilities and realities of the spiritual world.

Uzi's transcendentalism, which he employs to make Erie know himself beyond the spiritual realm becomes very vital to the understanding of the book: "You do not conquer death; you live life" (190). Ce uses themes that connect reality with the spiritual realm in an attempt to further complicate the modernist temperament of his novel. For a novel to be modern and worth reading, it must explore that which is above the material world. Ce's main concern in the novel seems to be the inner workings of Erie, his thought processes, and how he engages the world surrounding him. He can only engage the world surrounding him through memory, hence Jean-Paul Sartre, states that, "the past takes on a sort of super reality; its contours are hard and clear, unchangeable" (89).

This struggle to comprehend the distinction between the internal and external surroundings does not affect Erie only, but also his spiritual-genetic double Deego, because what he experiences in the subconscious seems to be real, since the dream girl in his subconscious and Sarah seem to be the same. This struggle of the perception of reality permeates the novel. In the words of Virginia Woolf: "whether we call it life or spirit, truth or reality, this, the essential thing, has moved off, or on, and refuses to be contained any longer in such ill-fitting vestments as we provide" (3). In essence, the gulf between the internal (soul) and the external (material world) is not navigable; hence, Erie, through the help of Uzi, removes the material binoculars which are responsible for his vertigo in the ancestral world. Immediately he breaks down the material barriers that bar him from knowing himself, he delves into the depths of his soul to find the spiritual, the truth. The barrier finally crumbles only through memory.

A more intriguing aspect of *The Visitor* is the fascinating concept of human interaction. Characters in the novel are being continually merged together through their own imaginations and memories. The two interesting examples are the relationship between Mensa, Erie and Deego on the one hand and that between Zeta, Sena and Sarah on the other. It would seem that Erie sees Mensa physically, but he never visually sees him; yet Mensa is the most significant part of him. Neither does Deego encounter his other selves physically. Ce clearly merges these characters together and blurs the lines a little. The Zeta-Sena-Sarah character is also difficult to link yet we know we are dealing with the same entity. Says Virginia Woolf: "life is not a series of gig lamps symmetrically arranged; life is a luminous halo, a semi-transparent envelope surrounding us from the beginning of consciousness to the end" (4). And similarly, Hillis Miller avers: "no man or woman is limited to him or herself, but each is joined to the others, diffused like a mist among all the people and places he or she has encountered"(173). The characters in Chin Ce's novel are indeed connected on various levels and Ce shows the connection quite acutely through the eyes of Deego.

The Visitor is very similar to Joel Silver's movie *Matrix*. Its structure and thematic drive is not far from the film. In both the novel and the film, the heroes' body and mind are separated. The protagonist of the film does not only possess a double identity but also has two different names. He is known as Thomas Anderson in the software firm where he works as a programmer. However, when he orchestrates his illegal deals in the Internet and when in the 'matrix', he is addressed as Neo. The singular item which indisputably demonstrates the semblance of the texts is the use of the word déjà vu. It is used and applied in the same sense in both texts. Erie uses it as a sudden response to acknowledge his physical resemblance to Mensa. While Neo uses it to express his acknowledgement of two cats that are so similar. Just like Deego who can hardly draw the line between sleep and *'awakeness,'* when he comments that "the line between my sleep and waking states had been thin indeed" (196), so does Neo find it difficult to distinguish between reality and dream: "You ever have that feeling when you are quite not sure whether you are awake or still dreaming" (Silver *Matrix*).

Erie is assisted by Grandad and Uzi to know himself beyond what he knows of himself, since he is unable to recollect his past as result of the bullet he receives in his head before transcending into ancestral world. Neo, on the other hand, is assisted by Morpheus and the Oracle to see himself beyond his mortal limitations. However, both texts differ at the level of realism. Though both texts employ and imbue the features of science fiction, the novel seems to be more realistic in structure, especially as the protagonist oscillates between dream and *'awakeness'*. In this 'psychological geography' (the dream world) anything is possible and acceptable because the dream world defies most logical processes of nature such as linear time.

CHIN CE: TOWARD A POSTCOLONIAL AESTHETIC

In *The Visitor*, Ce returns to a consistent repertoire of common postcolonial themes. He critiques the ubiquity of corruption and violence in contemporary Nigeria, creates a voice for the *lowdowns* and most powerless members of the African society, and explores the ongoing cultural confrontation between foreign and indigenous traditions in postcolonial Africa. This way, Ce expands the scope of postcolonial African literature by augmenting its political engagement of social realism with the kind of aesthetic engagement found in many modernist texts. Although the ingenuity of Ce's narrative style is not in doubt, yet this is not new in African fiction. Ce particularly develops the rich imagination, complex mythical imagery, and episodic adventures that are also found in works like Amos Tutuola's *Palm-Wine Drinkard,* Gabriel Okara's *The Voice,* and D. O Fagunwa's Yoruba novels.

The effort to create literary forms modeled after the narrative strategies of the African oral traditions continues another important aspect of contemporary postcolonial African writing because it attempts to engage postcolonial aesthetic forms as well as socio-political issues. By this sense of redirecting his experimental energy towards an exploration of African models rather than European ones, Ce has tactically prepared himself for a new stage of aesthetic development. His ability to combine the technique of realism, modernism, and African oral traditions aptly substantiates the above claim. This is the kind of postcolonial aesthetic Homi Bhabha describes as "Cultural Hybridity", because it explores the liminal border between diverse cultural traditions:

> The borderline work of culture demands an encounter with 'newness' that is not part of the continuum of past and present. It creates a sense of the new as an insurgent act of cultural translation. Such art does not merely recall the past as social cause or aesthetic precedent; it renews the past, refiguring it as a contingent 'in-between' space that innovates and interrupts the performance of the present.(7)

The Visitor is a manifestation of Ce's mastery of realism, modernism and African mythical traditions, thereby demonstrating that these diverse cultural traditions can coexist within new hybrid forms. Although similar to the experimentation found in Ben Okri's *Astonishing the Gods* and Biyi Bandele-Thomas' *The Sympathetic Undertaker and other Dreams in* the sense of spiritual, mythical vision, *The Visitor* displays more political engagement and more experimental energy/complexity. Ce's characters are wholly developed; the narrative structure is complex yet lucid, and its mythical vision develops a high intensity because it is counterbalanced with a realistic dimension. Because of these attributes, one can establish that the book is racy, chatty and engagingly mythical with numerous filmic and photographic

149

delights, realized through suspense, numerous flash backs and foreshadowing. Through narratology Ce does not only attain structural cum-thematic balance, he utopianizes and reasserts the modernist injunction that fiction must be concerned with the reality of life, its inherent truth and spirituality.

If fiction is geared only towards the exploration of the material, its functionality will be limited to the service of humanity, because there is a world beyond the material that begs to be explored. In *The Visitor*, Ce explores this other world, and brings to light fascinating possibilities that lie far beyond the realms of the material. And if modernism was a paradigm shift for the West, for Chin Ce it constitutes a paradigm extension. Ce does not simply imitate existing standards. Like any good artist, he recreates the old, stamping it with his very own artistic *label*.

WORKS CITED

Achebe, Chinua. *Morning Yet on Creation Day*. London: Heineman, 1975.

Alteri, Charles. *Painterly Abstraction in Modernist American Poetry*. New York: Cambridge UP, 1989.

Bhabha, Homi. *The Location of Culture*. New York: Routledge, 1994

Bradbury, Malcolm and M'Farlane, James (ed) *Modernism*. London: Penguin, 1976.

Ce, Chin. "The Art of Younger Poets". *New Voices: A Collection of recent Poetry from Nigeria*. Ed. GMT Emezue. IRCALC 2003 15 Mar. 2007 < http://www.africaresearch.org/ NvIntro.htm>.

− − −. *The Visitor*. Lagos: Handel Books, 2005.

Friedman, Allan. "The Novel". *The Twentieth Century Mind: History, Ideas and Literature in Britain*. Ed. Cox C. B. and A. E. Cox, London: Oxford, UP, 1972.

Grants, Amanda "Memory, Transition and Dialogue: The Cyclic Order of Chin Ce's Oeuvres". *Journal of African Literature and Culture.* Ed. Smith Charles, 2006. 11 29.

Hewit, Douglas. *English Fiction of the Early Modern Period 1890 1940.* New York: Longman, 1988.

Ker, David. *The African Novel and the Modernist Tradition.* Ibadan: Mosuro Publishers, 2003.

Lenser, Susan. *The Narrative Act: Point of View in Prose Fiction.* New Jersey: Princeton University Press, 1981.

Muton, Alan. *Fredric James: Fables of Aggression.* Santa Barbara: Black Sparrow Press, 1984.

Miller, J. Hillis. "Repetition as Raising the Dead". *Virginia Woolf.* Ed. Harold Bloom. New York: Chelsea, 1986.

Nnolim, Charles. "Trends in the Nigerian Novel". *Literature and National Consciousness.* Ed. Ernest Emenyonu. Calabar: Heineman, 1989.

Ojaide, Tanure. "New Trends in Modern African Poetry". *Research in African Literatures.* Ed. Abiola Irele, Vol. 26, No. 1, 1995. 4-19.

Ortega, Y. Gasset, Jose. "The Dehumanization of Arts". *The Idea of the Modern.* Ed. Irving Howe. New York: Horizon Press, 1967.

Reid, Panthea. "The Scene of Writing and the Shape of Language for Faulkner When Matisse and Picasso Yet Painted". *Faulkner and the Artist.* Jackson, Miss: U of Miss P.1986.

Sartre, Jean Paul. "On the Sound and the Fury: Time in the Work of Faulkner". *A Collection of Critical Essays.* Ed. Robert Penn Warren Englewood Cliffs, New Jersey: Prentice Hall, 1966. (87-93).

Silver, Joel. dir. *Matrix.* Perf. Keanu Reeves, Laurence Fisburne and Carrie-Anne Moss, 1999. Videocasette. Warner Bros. Home Video, 1999.

Warren, Beck. "William Faulkner's Style". *Four Decades of Criticism.* Ed. Linda Wagner. Lansing: University of Michigan, 1973.

Woolf, Virginia. "Modern Fiction". *The Common Reader.* New York: Harcourt, Brace and Co., 1925. 207-2 18.

Poetry

8

Subjectificatory Structures
POETRY 'IN THE SEASON OF ANOTHER LIFE'
G. A. R. Hamilton

*L*ike the works of many other politically-conscious Nigerian poets
–such as Ada Ugah, Odia Ofeimun, and Niyi Osundare– Chin
Ce's collection of poetry, *An African Eclipse*, is clearly concerned
with the ethical and moral transgressions of Nigeria's political
leaders in its post-independence years. Yet, one would like to
demonstrate here how Ce's poetry offers something more profound
than a simple sketch of the various past injustices inflicted on a
largely poor Nigerian population by both civilian and military
leaders following the official end of British colonial governance.
Indeed, this paper argues that Ce's *An African Eclipse* conceptualises
a non-personal force of Life that not only conditions a revolutionary
way of being for its readers but also functions as an ethical principle
that has the potential to become the antidote to the diseased morality
of Nigeria's political leaders.

In a little-known article on the work of Jean-Paul Sartre,
GillesDeleuze laments 'the sadness of generations without teachers'
(77). It is a sentiment that finds its conceptual correlate in the
frustration that characterises Chinua Achebe's criticism of post-
independence Nigerian leadership. 'The Nigerian problem', Achebe

writes, 'is the unwillingness or inability of its leaders to rise to the responsibility, to the challenge of personal example which are the hallmarks of true leadership' (1). Given the context of a succession of corrupt civilian and military administrations, Achebe's frustration with the inability of Nigeria's leading political figures to assume the role of teacher to the nation seems entirely merited. But the concept of a teacher to the nation goes further than simply setting a good example for others to follow. 'Our teachers', Deleuze continues, are those who find 'ways of thinking that correspond to our modernity'. That is to say, our teachers are those people who can find ways of thinking that are not antiquated or antithetical to our present situation – those that are mindful of our 'difficulties as well as our vague enthusiasms' that we experience in life (77).

For Ce, this simply cannot be said of the post-independence Nigerian political leaderships. Indeed, the political emphasis of Ce's *An African Eclipse* ensures that the collection is not without (many) examples of the impoverished condition of what one might call 'State thinking'. So, Ce writes of the profligacy of political administrations and the manner in which such recklessness and wastefulness is learned and repeated by the Nigerian everyman in the damning social commentary of 'Prodigal Drums'; he writes of the rampant egoism of Nigeria's political leaders in 'African Eclipse', which results in the social blight of self-interest and self-importance and claims of billions of dollars in oil revenues siphoned from the Nigerian economy by some Nigerian leaders and their families; and he writes of the willingness of the politicians to hide, rather than disclose and resolve, social problems and injustices in the poems of 'The Second Reptile' and 'The Champ'. Taken in concert, Ce's cutting overview of State thinking presents a scathing indictment of a leadership that demonstrates a complete inability to empathise with, and react to, the experience of being a modern Nigerian. However, in Ce's essay 'Bards and Tyrants' one can trace the inability of the political leadership to form an appreciation of other Nigerians to a failure of thinking itself. Linked to his discussion of the degeneration of the integrity of the Nigerian university system, Ce reasons that the inadequacy of State thinking is due to the failure of Nigeria's political class to engage in deep personal thought at the hands of a 'liberating' literature:

> Nigeria's political elite do not care for literature or any book for that matter... there is hardly any hope that its liberating thought can ever coalesce in the form of a liberating philosophy... Insights garnered from the literatures of their brightest minds have been ignored. (2005)

As such, one is forced to conclude that the State's inability to adopt a way of thinking that reflects the experience of being a modern Nigerian is just that –*an inability*. That is to say, the repugnant social effects of an impoverished State thought, which Ce outlines in his poetry, are not the consequence of choice but of true ignorance. With the deterioration in the standards of formal education institutions, the operation of a 'personal thought' that can account for social justice withdraws to leave a vacuum that is filled by an unbridled individualism. Such individualism leads to a blindness to social ills, to a blindness to bony-headed 'Children/On the streets' (*'An African Eclipse*' 15-16) and to a deafness to the 'cries of torture and murder' that 'sweep the streets' (40-41). Indeed, such individualism cannot offer a way of thinking that corresponds to the difficulty of enduring both the painful lived experience of the ethically and morally bankrupt national leadership and the passion engendered in the promise of self-rule, free from British colonial control. Left unchecked, the Nigerian Everyman only stands to inherit this caustic individualism which erodes the very pathways to a social consciousness that is demanded by political contestation. Simply put, without access to some kind of teaching that can proliferate creative personal thought, the adoption of such individualism can only result in an unchallenged procession of dictatorial administrations.

Clearly, such a situation is morally, ethically, and politically unacceptable. And it is for this reason that there is a necessity to

157

reposition the role of the teacher. Under such conditions, the role of the teacher must migrate from the shoulders of politicians to the figure of the writer. As South-African novelist and academic J.M. Coetzee notes in response to André Brink, the writer must become the medical diagnostician of the State (Coetzee 1990), ensuring that clinical and critical faculties intersect in order to diagnose, at the very least, the psychological condition of the State. Yet, it is also important to note that Brink's ideas can only come to fruition if, in the words of Achebe, the African writer takes on the role of the teacher:

> The worst thing that can happen to any people is the loss of their dignity and self-respect. The writer's duty is to help them regain it by showing them in human terms what happened to them, what they lost...In Africa he cannot perform this task unless he has a proper sense of history.(7)

There are two highly important features to note about Achebe's assertion, here; and both are granted considerable attention in Ce's *An African Eclipse*. Firstly, one must recognise that what Achebe promotes in this passage is a programme of recovery by which every Nigerian person can reclaim the act of self-determination. In this programme, the role of the writer is to render visible the apparatuses of subjectification (those structures that facilitate the loss of 'dignity and self-respect' to which Achebe refers) which condition the individual as a passive, State-governed entity who is unable to enter into any kind of revolutionary activity by appealing to 'a proper sense of history'. So, it is perhaps unsurprising that, as though in direct response to Achebe's call, Ce organises his poems in *An African Eclipse* through a tripartite division of time that leans heavily towards the historical – the past (twenty-one poems), the present (the singular opening poem), and the future (the four concluding poems of the collection). However, it is significant that Ce's artificial temporal divisions are not strictly adhered to. Indeed, one need only reflect on the fact that the poem that opens the collection, 'A Farewell – 'the single poem dedicated to the present – is continually informed by the poems that follow it to understand the importance that Ce ascribes to both the past and the future in the constitution of the present. For example, the sympathetic narrator of 'A Farewell' reminds an unnamed partner:

> We saw lined behind the gloom
> Only our own graffiti
> (And phantoms loomed) ahead. (8-10)

The notion of 'graffiti', here, takes on an added significance once the reader associates it with the 'scorched earth' discussed in the later poem 'The Second Reptile' which stands as the result of the Biafran conflict of the late 1960s and the unheeded but continuing erosion affecting the eastern regions of Nigeria, described in 'Windstorm'. Upon reading these, what might usefully be termed, 'poems-of-the-past', the unanchored reference to graffiti in 'A Farewell' becomes indicative of a human violence so grotesque that it inscribes the very earth; a human violence so monstrous that it produces a permanent physical and incorruptible record of past injustices and discrimination perpetuated by an unthinking political class on the Nigerian people; a human violence, Ce tells the reader which even the progress symbolised by a nation of skyscrapers cannot hide ('The Second Reptile'). Yet, vitally, this violent act of inscribing the earth (a literal geo-graphism/geography) captured in the simplicity of the term 'graffiti' begins to haunt the 'looming phantoms ahead' –each of the decisions that the Nigerian people must make when postulating the nation's strides into a progressive future. Suddenly, references to geography, to 'the still waters' mentioned in 'Blessings' and the mountains and fields of 'Eagle', invoke the spectre of a past that carries a multitude of warnings for the future. This is why even in his most optimistic of political poems, Ce cautions his readers to 'Watch guard on the mountain' against ambitions that 'may lurk in dark corners/Of the mind' ('Eagle': 11-13).

Undoubtedly, the manner in which the different temporalities of the past, present, and future continually reflect and penetrate each other produces a complex conceptualisation of time that reveals, to use Ce's own words, 'the run of history' (*Full Moon* iii). Indeed, it is in developing an appreciation of this 'run of history' that one can begin to see how Ce's difficult conceptualisation of time is directly associated to the second feature of Achebe's assertion. For it is not just the intricate relationships between the divergent temporalities of past, present, and future that produce 'the run of history' but also the way in which private experiences and publicly accepted 'truths' intersect and pervert each other. With this in mind, one must take careful note of the ethical position that Achebe promotes in this passage since it is the same ethical position that Ce adopts in his political poetry.

For Achebe, it is clear that there is a certain ethical position that the writer must assume in order to fulfil the role of teacher. The writer/teacher must enter into a close relationship with the reader so that the reader can begin the restorative process of understanding 'what happened to them, what they lost' ('The Role' 7). It is an ethical position that is premised on the deep appreciation of the other: the writer's respect for the reader, and the reader's respect for the writer. Moreover, the force of this necessary ethical relationship that describes the nexus of the revolutionary writer and reader is only doubled by the recognition that the lost personal qualities of dignity and self-respect, to which Achebe refers, can only function when placed in direct relation to the social. Nowhere is a dependence and reliance on the social –that is, on 'other people'– more profound than in a consideration of history. And it is this fact, that history demands some semblance of community before it can be said to hold any value, which seems to be the reason why Achebe settles on 'a proper sense of history' as the key thematic concern of every writer/teacher. In such a context, it is certain that an important quality of the writer/teacher is the ability to compose access points to a history that possesses the potential to facilitate the reader's ideological migration from a destructive individualism to an ethical entryway into the social.

As such, if it is true that Ce aims to produce a revolutionary literature as a writer/teacher that helps the Nigerian people restore some kind of self-determinism in the wake of the demise of colonial structures of subjectification, then his primary role must remain the development of an ethical position –a position formalised, that is, by a deep appreciation and recognition of the importance of all others. Thus the role of the writer/teacher calls first for the ability to render visible structures of subjectification in order to make them a target for revolutionary activity, and then, following the demise of such structures, for the ability to propagate the immanent integrity of the everyman by encouraging acts of self-determination born from the ethically-charged event of a deep respect for others.

Of course, Ce's *An African Eclipse* demonstrates both of these properties. Ce assumes the role of teacher by producing a political poetry that not only reveals the means by which the Nigerian everyman lost his dignity, self-respect, and sense of history, but also recognises and details the intricate relationship between the individual and society. Played out in a dialogue held between painful personal experiences of the past and the liberatory promise of the future, Ce's poetry encourages a valuable reappraisal of the self that has the potential to lead to social revolution at the hands of a politically informed people. Yet, importantly, I want to suggest that these two properties –the necessity of the writer to render visible structures of subjectification and the necessity of the writer to engage in the ethically-charged event of crystallising a deep recognition and appreciation of others– are linked in a very particular way in *An African Eclipse* by a concept of 'Life' that exists as a separate force beyond the individual.

Writing on the complex relationship between the private and public worlds of the poet and society, Ce states, 'this flow of inner and outer worlds complements the creative nature of soul as synonymous with self-dreaming' (*Full Moon* iii). It is an enigmatic remark that pushes the reader, perhaps too gently, towards a particular way of engaging with his poetry. Nevertheless, the diligent reader is encouraged to reconsider the notion that stands at the very heart of *An African Eclipse*– the soul. It is clear that Ce is trying to negotiate some kind of union between the metaphysical soul and the very physical aspects of the self, here. But, what is not so clear is how Ce thinks of this union coming into being. Under examination, the significance of the relationship between the soul and the act of 'the soul' of Ce's poetry, with all of the connotations it takes from Christian tradition at this point, becomes inextricable from the very principle of life itself and necessarily ceases to 'belong' to any discrete entity since it must always remain a non-personal 'principle'. Thus, it should come as no surprise that one's introduction to Ce's notion of the soul arrives via this curious incorporeal order of Life that, in standing apart from the individual, has the power to inaugurate the dawning of each new day:

> I have chosen now the day is bright
> (the shining light of
> soul lights) the middle lonely route.
> (14-16)

So, Ce begins his collection of political poems by demonstrating the force of this somewhat mystical quality of the soul, or rather this curious non-personal principle of Life, which makes manifest the very possibility of the day(light). Clearly, this concept of Life exists as an independent force to the individual; but it is also made equally clear elsewhere that the individual must subsist within its domain or suffer the consequences. In 'Darkness', Ce laments about 'A generation without a soul' (9) –a generation which, from the notes appended to the collection, one is encouraged to read as the Nigerian military class since 1966. Without a soul, without access to this non-personal force of Life, the military class 'sent the nation/Blundering in the dark' ('Darkness' 1-2). Indeed, Nigeria's dive into 'darkness' at the hands of corrupt political leaders is a theme that Ce returns to time and again in 'An African Eclipse', 'May 29 1999', 'Darkness Broods', and so on.

Importantly, however, such a dive into darkness is repeatedly attributed to the failure in the relationship forged between the personal and non-personal world, which necessarily issues from this ubiquitous force of Life. Put simply, Ce's poems recognise that such a non-personal force of Life functions as an ethical principle; and, moreover, that it is this ethical principle that guarantees the manner in which we conduct ourselves. As such, Ce's singular notion of an independent force of Life functions as a means to evaluate what we do, say, think, and feel according to the kind of ontological condition that each of these activities implies.

Here, then, lies the significance of Ce's conceptualisation of this non-personal force of Life –it is another kind of Life, written as the soul, which allows Ce as writer/teacher to render visible all kinds of structures of subjectification by returning to history's lessons, to encourage a deep recognition and respect for others and in so doing raise the potential for revolutionary activity at the hands of a socially and politically informed people. 'In the season of another life' ('Eagle'), Ce's poetry leads a 'new' people to a position where they have the potential to socially and politically re-engineer Nigeria by overturning the practices and apparatuses of a corrupt national leadership that is characterised by its failed ethical and moral responsibilities to the Nigerian population.

Ce is quick to highlight one of the least commonly recognised structures for the subjectification, or subjugation, of the Nigerian people. In just the third poem of his collection, Ce renders visible the means by which corrupt presidential figures and administrations stole the self-respect and dignity of a generation of Nigerian workers. Highlighting the media networks that continually channelled government propaganda to the people, 'The Champ' talks of the duplicitous dealings of trickster presidents with quick fingers that rifle the national oil revenue for personal gain:

> Every now fulsomely
> flashed his many faces
> at national networks.
> Octopus and green his
> hands
> around a hundred contracts. (1-6)

And, given Ce's observations in poems such as 'Darkness Broods' and 'African Eclipse', the reader is made further aware that this already unacceptable state of affairs is only doubled by a rehearsed and empty rhetoric on social and economic injustices that 'Tumble from liquorice throats' ('Darkness Broods' 8):

> Fine speeches and stale State
> Declarations
> With presidential pretences
> On your face.
> There sprawl forgotten bearers
> Of the land's loads.
> You do not see their eyes
> And the bony heads of their
> Children
> On the streets   (7-16)

Through this kind of political 'education' at the hands of incumbent politicians serving their time at state-sanctioned television stations, the Nigerian everyman is reduced to a most passive entity in the eyes of a military leadership, a kind of 'snivelling vermin' ('The Second Reptile' 15). Perhaps it is this impoverished conceptualisation of the Nigerian population that accounts for the ease with which violent acts have been perpetrated upon it. For Ce makes clear that the operation of subjectification that pacifies the minds of the Nigerian people is matched by an operation of subjectification that conditions the physical body. Thus, 'Ovation' recalls 'the chilling violence' (20) committed by Nigerian military rulers on their way to political power, which resulted in the common Nigerian being further isolated from the political system; and, 'An African Eclipse' evokes the 'cries of torture and murder' that swept the streets where the 'mad dogs', or gangs of enforcers, roamed the streets (40-42) –if not killing, then routinely humiliating and degrading people. It is a programme of violence that results in what Ce quite rightly observes as a measure of bodily limitation, of bondage. Under such means of physical oppression the Nigerian population is left:

Tired and drawn
We trotted the streets
Among a black throng
Without a human face.

Our eyes may be blank
Like drops of phlegm
And sightless
As the dead's…
Who wants to know? ('Chains': 1-11)

So, the reader is forced to record a pacification of the people, a loss of singularity in the context of a collapse of social relationships and responsibility that ultimately results in the kind of blindness to "Many loveless hearts /And other drab minds" –the benefits of political engagement that allows dictatorships to proliferate. Indeed, Ce details a particularly impressionable and compliant State-governed individual. Yet, while it is certain that such an individual is capable of reproducing learned violent behaviour –such as witnessed in the poem 'A Cloud'– it is also absolutely certain that such an individual is unable to employ such behaviour in any kind of organised revolutionary way. As such, it is unsurprising to find a poem included in the collection that draws attention to the problem of black African fighting against black African, even in the face of what most recognise as a clear political triumph –the freeing of Nelson Mandela from a South African jail in 1990:

What justice
That sped the flaming
Wing of the eagle
Through the fire and splatter
of hell now blinds
Our black brothers' eyes?
What cry of soul
Can pierce Nelson's dark cloud

Of black against brother?   ('A Cloud': 21-29)

However, at the root of this kind of unthinking violence, which Ce admits belongs as much to Nigeria as it does South Africa, Ce identifies a largely unacknowledged legacy of British colonial rule. The poem 'Naija' gestures towards a forgotten history, a history that saw the British compose the boundaries of what was to become the nation-state of Nigeria.

> Pretend this is Nigeria
> North or South Left or Centre, Forward
> Backward   ('Naija': 9-11)

Undoubtedly, such an act of inscription, which Britain engaged in during the 'Scramble for Africa' with other European colonial powers, began a process of homogenisation that necessarily collapsed the territorial distinction between different ethnic and cultural groups of the West African region, and resulted in the kind of disorientation that Ce alludes to above: 'North or South Left or Centre, Forward' (10). However, it would be wrong to attribute the violence and political turmoil experienced by Nigeria to this common European desire for a singular nation-state.   Indeed, rather than pointing the finger at the British colonial administration responsible for fabricating the borders of a new Nigeria, Ce seems more concerned with highlighting what many regard as the deeply flawed political system that fails to provide a suitable framework for the equal representation of ethnic groups that Britain devised upon its official departure from the territory. And it is this flawed political system, which ultimately favours the Hausa/Fulani populations of the north over the Yoruba of the west and (especially) the Igbo of south-eastern Nigeria, which urges Ce to ask:

> What further curse of the
> Triangle
> Awaits your children, folks,
> If you let them...   (14-17)

Significantly, Ce renders visible this legacy of colonial control as a contemporary structure of subjectification, a political system that still dominates and conditions Nigerian life, that is ripe for either revision or revolution.

Yet, it is most important that Ce does not see this problematic political system as the only legacy of colonialism. Hand in hand with an imported European political system that presumed some kind of majoritarian notion of nationalism, was the development of a truly national economy that pulled people from rural to urban areas to meet the needs of the capitalist marketplace. Unfortunately, the consequence of such social movement, a production economy, and the demands made on the environment by the discovery of huge oil fields in the 1970s, was an ecological damage that has not only scarred the natural landscape but also the consciousness of many Nigerian writers, such as Nnimo Bassey and Niyi Osundare. Somewhat disheartened at the processes of desertification and erosion that have continually gone unheeded by various state and federal governments, Ce remarks on a modernity that ranges:

> From the wastelands of the Savannah
> Through the craters of the Niger...
> (12-13)

For Ce, then, the truth of modernity is found in the scarred earth, in the continual processes of penetration and erosion that find their conceptual correlate in the continuing penetration and erosion of traditional values and practices at the hands of 'modernity':

> Clouds and sands and stormy
> Wind whirl over our land
> We are no longer at ease
> As things have fallen apart. (1-4)

Ce is clearly sympathetic to Achebe's ideas in *The Trouble with Nigeria* (1984), a work to which the poem 'Windstorm' is dedicated.

However, for Ce, it seems as though a remedy to the social and political difficulties that face the modern Nigerian cannot be found in hasty calls for Nigeria to simply 'modernise'. Indeed, the reference to two of Achebe's more prophetic novels here *No Longer at Ease* (1960) and *Things Fall Apart* (1958) –which both concern the decrepitude of traditional values in the face of the colonial encounter seems to highlight this very point. Where Achebe's novels appear to demand (yet always seem to fail to deliver) a singular leader of the people, Ce reminds his readership that they need not await the equivalent of a 'sage on silent feet' ('Windstorm' 20) in order to undertake revolutionary activity. While the possibility engendered by a future that always resides at a crossroads between the recollection of traditional practices and the progress ensured through innovation may not be arrived at through the 'measured strides' of a singular leader with a clear and purposeful vision, nonetheless the promise of innovation will be realised by a people who struggle for it. Simply, it is 'the people' who must engage in a process whereby they enter into a deep recognition of others around themselves in order to become a revolutionary force. Importantly, this idea of becoming begins to play an increasingly significant role in the poetry of Chin Ce. As a present participle, becoming refuses to hierarchise, privilege, or determine discrete points in time since it recognises that every living entity is in a continuing moment of change, undergoing perpetual movement. Thus the process of becoming is always and already a revolutionary movement since it is a movement, Ce recognises, which can only distort or pervert State-approved ways of living. What this means is that Ce challenges his readers in his poetry to deny the State's authority to commit ethically and morally repugnant acts with impunity: the acts of violence written in 'Ovation'; the demonstrated ignorance of economic and social issues that forms the fabric of 'An African Eclipse'; the manipulation of the news media for overt political purposes in 'Darkness Broods'; and the continued use of the dilapidated colonial legal and administrative apparatuses witnessed in 'Prodigal Drums'. As such, for the revolutionary potential of the people to be realised the people themselves must first inhabit a position, a way of being, which is outside of those sanctioned by the State: to challenge the structures of subjectification such as those Ce highlights, to become what might usefully be called a 'private thinker' someone who can draw on their own knowledge of the past to compose their own future rather than a person who is content to passively accept State assertions of 'the Truth'. So it is that the poetry of Ce calls for an awareness of self that is built upon the process of becoming, a process that recalls all the complexity of the ethical relationship to the Other since it resides within the communion between the liquid sites of past and future as they play themselves out in the present encounter between the inner personal world of the poet and the outer public world of the Other

Together with Ce's claim that this 'flow of inner and outer worlds complements the creative nature of soul as synonymous with self-dreaming' (*Full Moon* iii), the reader is presented with the building blocks to a very specific understanding of the composition of a modern Nigerian ontology. It is as if Ce locates our only political way of existing in the world through the production of the literary artefact. It is a position that Gilles Deleuze has developed throughout his oeuvre. For Deleuze:

> writing is a question of becoming, always incomplete, always in the midst of being formed, and goes beyond the matter of any livable or lived experience. It is a process, that is, a passage of Life that traverses both the livable and the lived. (Deleuze 1)

Given such an understanding, it is certain that every literary work must imply a way of being which is to say, a form of Life. Yet, while the act of writing is an acceptable revolutionary activity in itself, it must be noted that the kind of Life, or the way of living, that writings such as *An African Eclipse* imply for its readership results in an equally revolutionary force. By understanding 'a proper sense of history', to return to Achebe's phrase, which reveals the structures of subjectification that condition the minds and bodies of the Nigerian population, Ce's readers become private thinkers who begin to inhabit a revolutionary space that is positioned in order to compromise the integrity of State-organised ontologies. It is a process of becoming revolutionary that insists on a new awareness of the self, a self-interrogation that demands not only a reappraisal of the world but also the way in which one engages with it. But, while such acts of introspection always carry the threat of being narcissistic, egoistic or more worryingly, nihilistic because of the potential to fall into an irretrievable solipsism, Ce makes certain that one understands that:

> In this awareness of self, both poet and reader are running through time, defying the lower pulls of gravity including the outer world filled with limitation of doctrines, political power and the abuses of it which transience underlines its illusions in the infinite passage of time. (*Full* iii)

Running through time together, exploring history through the lens of today, at a speed that defies the processes of subjectification, Ce seems at pains to explain that the poet and reader are held in an inextricable relationship, a moment of becoming that eradicates the distance between the poet and reader. Bound in such a communion born of the 'highest ethical sense' ('Blessings' 12), it is impossible that the kind of introspection that Ce's poetry requests of its readers can ever result in a nihilistic dive into solipsism. Indeed, Ce is so careful in explaining that the process of writing survives on the interaction of writer and reader that it is perhaps unsurprising that the first word of the first poem of *An African Eclipse* is 'we' –a gesture that not only underscores the principle of unity that runs throughout Ce's poetry but also one that recognises the significance of something other to oneself:

> We met where three ways
> were laid
> between thick forests   (1-2)

In this ethically-charged environment where poet and reader

begin to coalesce, writing can no longer claim to be an activity that attains a discrete form since it must always already be infused with the 'incomprehensibility' of the reader. Indeed, as Deleuze argues, writing can only be an activity that at best attempts to find 'a zone of proximity' to the haecceities that constitute the singularity of any subject. As such, literature must insistently claim to be an act of creation, it must invent the possibility of Life and with it new ways of existing (Deleuze 100). So Deleuze goes on to talk of the need for political literature to 'create a new people', a new collective, a new readership that is formalised by its encounter with the newly produced revolutionary text. In such a manner, the moment of becoming between Chin Ce and his readership that is produced through the revolutionary character of his poetry ultimately facilitates new ways of being a modern Nigerian. Under such conditions, it is no longer profitable to think of the writer as one who simply represents experience through writing, which is to say a writer *for* or *on the behalf of* a people. Rather, the writer must be considered as an inextricable element of the people, to all intents and purposes inseparable from the people, who, in refusing to simply represent personal experiences, creates non-preexistent relations between poets, readers, and the process of becoming revolutionary, in order to demonstrate new possibilities of Life –new ways of living within a new Nigeria.

Nowhere is this revised treatment of the role of the writer/teacher to society better evidenced than in the enigmatic poem 'Oracle':

> The one in the sacred grove
> Is he
> Who can see
> The jaws of the red ant.
> ...
> The one in the sacred grove
> Is only me.
> Is only you...   (1-4 and 15-17)

It is important to note here the ability of the narrator (poet) to see new things, new moments of life, the impossible detail of the 'jaws of the red ant', with all the implications of a poet-as-oracle who has the ability to regard features of the world that others pass by unwittingly. Without further inspection of the poem one is left wondering whether this is Ce claiming to be a writer *for* the people, the disseminator of an almost unseen and therefore mysterious knowledge. But Ce introduces a certain complexity to this understanding by insisting that the enunciation of 'only me' holds exactly the same value as 'only you'. Suddenly, the poem is no longer about Ce claiming to possess an arcane understanding of the world; it becomes a poem that demonstrates that Ce, and everything he writes, is inextricable from his reader and bound by an ethical contract. Since the differentiation implied by 'I' and 'You' necessarily loses all critical value under such conditions, it must be replaced with the use of a third person singular that *cannot* be used to isolate or marginalise a subject from an object because, quite simply, it does not inaugurate the hierarchical binary system required by 'I' and 'You'. In this extraordinary 'middle voice' that navigates between the demands of subjects and objects, of absolutes and essentialisms, of Self and Other, Ce's poetry stands as the emission of a collective utterance, a pure speech act, which allows a new revolutionary people 'to find their expression in and through the singularity of the writer'. (Deleuze xiv) – *An African Eclipse*, that is, as an enunciation *of* the people merely produced through the singularity of the poet.

Let us conclude by invoking the unheard voice that seems to haunt Chin Ce's political poetry and, indeed, this paper. The words of Jean-Paul Sartre are always insightful and inventive, and this passage taken from his seminal text *What is Literature?* captures the very essence of not only the issues that Ce's *An African Eclipse* addresses but also the reason why it must address them:

> The writer takes up the world as is, totally raw, stinking, and quotidian, and presents it to free people on a foundation of freedom...It is not enough to grant the writer the freedom to say

whatever he pleases! He must address a public that has the freedom to change everything, which implies, beyond the suppression of social classes, the abolition of all dictatorship, the perpetual renewal of categories, and the continual reversal of every order, as soon as it starts to ossify. In a word, literature is essentially the subjectivity of a society in permanent revolution. (Sartre 162-163)

In short, it is a call for the writer to become a teacher: to recall the 'raw, stinking, and quotidian' real world and present an uncompromising literature that, because of its ethically-charged access to the world, has the potential to 'free people on a foundation of freedom' itself. Indeed, it is in this spirit that one leaves the last word to the enthusiasm and the promise of possibility engendered in the final poem of *An African Eclipse*:

> And when the thick, dun smoke
> Has dispersed
> Mournfully in the dark clouds.
> And the dusts have settled on the fields...
>
> Let your gaze sweep the fields
> Where the trees bear new fruits
> In the season of another life.

WORKS CITED

Achebe, Chinua 'The Role of the Writer in a New Nation' *African Writers on African Writing* (Ed.) D.G. Killam. London: Heinemann, 1973.
——— *The Trouble with Nigeria* Enugu: Fourth Dimension, 1984.
——— *No Longer at Ease* Nairobi: East African Educational Publishers, 1960.
Adewale, Toyin *Naked Testimonies* Lagos: Mace Books, 1995.
Ce, Chin 'Bards and Tyrants: Literature, Leadership and Citizenship Issues of Modern Nigeria' *Africa Literary Journal* B5 2005. 5-24.
———. *Full Moon: Selected Poems 1984-1992*. Enugu: Handel Books, 2001.

–––. *An African Eclipse and Other Poems*. Enugu: Handel Books, 2000.

Coetzee, J.M. 'André Brink and the Censor'. *Research in African Literature.* 21 (Fall), 1990.

–––. *Desert Islands and Other Texts:* 1953-1974. New York: Semiotext[e], 2004.

– – –. *Essays Critical and Clinical*. Trans. Daniel W. Smith and Michael Greco. London: Verso, 1998.

– – –. *Negotiations:* 1972-1990. Trans. Martin Joughin. New York: Columbia University Press, 1995.

Deleuze, Gilles and Félix Guattari. *What is Philosophy?* Trans. Hugh Tomlinson and Graham Burchell. New York: Columbia University Press, 1994.

Ofeimun, Odia. *The Poet Lied*. London: Longman Drumbeat, 1980.

Osundare, Niyi. *Songs of the Market Place*. Ibadan: New Horn, 1983.

Sartre, Jean-Paul. *Qu'est-ce que la literature?* Paris: Librairie Gallimard, 1948.

Ugah, Ada. *The Ballad of the Unknown Soldier*. Enugu: Harris Publishers, 1989.

9

History and Identity

DEREK WALCOTT'S AND CHIN CE'S POETRY

Agbor, Sarah Anyang

Amoah, Ama B.

*T*his paper compares some historical and racial constructions of identity in selected poems of the afro Caribbean poet, Derek Walcott and African poet Chin Ce. The literary creativity of a writer represents the cultures and traditions of the people as well as exposes the society's tensions and conflicts. Significantly, the experiences of post colonialism in Africa and afro Caribbean can be traced in poetic representations. This is so because the nature of history – an account of past events; or his/story – is evoked through memory and language always within the socio-cultural, religious, economic and political realities that inform the writer's society. Contemporary creative literatures of the once colonized can be considered revisionist literature that presents colonial legacies, postcolonial corruption and the conditions of their society. Contemporary West Indian and African poetry have thus become a means of historicizing history, remembering history and documenting the political and cultural experiences a people. This study points to the function of poetry, to educate, entertain, and moralize and sometimes ridicule. It compares attempts by Derek Walcott (afro Caribbean) and Chin Ce (Nigerian) to deploy elements of history, race and memory in their poetic works.

Derek Walcott is one of the best known, English-speaking Caribbean writers. He is also a renowned playwright and theatrical producer while Chin Ce, also a novelist, can be pitched in the third generation of Nigerian poets. The poetry of this generation is characterised by gory pictures of social contradictions that are sometimes resolved in favour of the masses. History and identity are manipulated by African and afro Caribbean writers in their creative imagination whether drama, poetry or prose. Selections from Derek Walcott's "The Estranging Sea", "The Sea Is History" and "A Far Cry from Africa" and Chin Ce's "Oracle" and "Clay gods" in An African Eclipse are some of both poets' signatures to the political and economic crises of their respective societies. In this study, we would examine Walcott's and Ce's societies and cultures which have inspired their poetic renditions. This would involve the assessment of the social factors at work in a poem as well as the cultural elements present directly or indirectly in a poem. Sometimes satire, riddles and proverbs have been manipulated by Walcott and Ce in their poetic representations and transposed as a means of asserting identity as well as interrogating the existing conditions prevalent in their societies.

West Indian society was a slave society following the conquest of the indigenes. The history of slavery and colonialism is replete in "A Far Cry from Africa" and "The Estranging Sea." The poet persona in "The Sea Is History," rhetorically asks: "Where are your monuments, your battles, Martyrs?" "Where is your tribal memory?" Walcott ironically interpolates his poetry with references to the Bible so as to document the various stages of colonialism. He criticises colonial history in the Caribbean. The history of colonialism is linked to the ocean /sea which colonisers used as the route to the assimilation of the hinterland. Hence the personification" but the ocean kept turning blank pages/ looking for history" (26). Walcott most directly equates Port Royal to "Jonah" and questions "but where is your Renaissance?" (26). The renaissance is "locked in them sea sands/…where the men-o'-war floated down;" (26). What is more pertinent is that the atrocities where such that colonial past is compared to "Gomorrah" and "lamentations" (27). The poet's philosophical and creative writing interrogates Christianity and its impact on slavery. The poet refers to the crucifixion of Jesus through "…the spires/lancing the side of God/ as His son set, and that was the New Testament" (27). This new phase came with a different form of colonialism "white sisters clapping/ to the waves' progress/and that was Emancipation-jubilation" (27). This refers to the evangelisation process which the colonialists utilise to subvert the people. This independence brought with it the struggle but the different islands to be independent thus: "and then each rock broke into its own nation" (27). At the birth of independence citizens were expected to cast their civic duty: "then came the bullfrog bellowing for a vote. He critiques the leaders such as jetting ambassadors'…and the mantis, like khaki police/ and the furred caterpillars of judges/ examining each case closely (28). The hardships experienced by the masses in this neocolonialism are what really history is. This poem positions the West Indian historicity within the triple variants of identity, migration, and memory to indicate how these oral narratives symbolized hope and renewed possibilities for the future through a process of creative resistance.

Walcott captures imperial wreckage in Africa in their assimilation, conquest and assimilation of Africa in "A Far Cry from Africa". The Poem opens "A wind is ruffling the tawny pelt/

Of Africa... (702). The tragic predicament of colonialism is captured .Walcott historically represents the Kikuyu resistance of British colonialism through the simile;"...Kikuyu, quick as flies, /Batten upon the bloodstreams of the veldt / (702). As they resisted British imposition they were killed and their blood streams on the grassland of the Veldt. Consequently "Corpses are scattered through a paradise." Paradise becomes a metaphor for Africa before the intrusion of the imperial master. There is regret in the horrendous crimes committed by the legacy of imperial rule:" Only the worm, colonel of carrion, cries: /'Waste no compassion on these separate dead!'" (702). He conveys the enormous crime committed against Africa. Simon Gikandi's Writing in Limbo: Modernism and Caribbean Literature announces this chilling reminder: "Caribbean literature and Culture are haunted by the presence of the 'discoverer' and the historical moment he inaugurates" (1). The colonial masters instead focus on the justification of their redemptive role: "Statistics justify and scholars seize/ The salients of colonial policy" (702). This deaths means nothing to those whose lives have been wasted "What is that to the white child hacked in bed?" and those whose lives have been considered as disposable: "To savages, expendable as Jews?"(703). The rhetorical questions and comparison through the simile "...savages expendable as the Jews" highlight the impunity of the British in the death of the Africans term as "savages" hence like the Jews their lives are dispensable. Walcott articulates the predicament of the Jews. During the period of the Crusades to the Enlightenment the Jews were excluded "from England in 1290 and from France in 1306. In 1391, forced conversions began in Spain; in 1492 all remaining Jews were expelled" ("Encyclopedia par. 5). Consequently many of the exiles perished while others "found asylum in the Netherlands and in the Turkish possessions". The

German Jews, who experienced periodic expulsions throughout the 15th century, fled to Poland, where, they were subject to persecution. Between 1933, when the Nazis rose to power in Germany, and 1945, when Germany was defeated in World War II, the Jews faced persecution of unprecedented scope and violence; thousands were driven into exile and close to 6 million were systematically slaughtered in the Holocaust ("Jews" par.8). These deaths were the victims of Germany's deliberate and systematic attempt to annihilate the entire Jewish population of Europe, a plan Hitler called the "Final Solution" (Endlosung). The Jews were marked for systematic and total annihilation and were singled out for "Special Treatment" (Sonderbehandlung), which meant that Jewish men, women and children were to be methodically killed with poisonous gas ("History")

Walcott demonstrates that the imperial masters were callous in their exploitation and dispossession of the African people machinery of exploitation. Hence: The violence of beast on beast is read/ As natural law, but upright man/ Seeks his divinity by inflicting pain" (703). Here he makes a determined protest against the Masters. He compares them to beasts through the simile "Delirious as these worried beasts, his wars/ Dance to the tightened carcass of a drum," and it is his power to kill over the native that the imperialist "calls courage" and his peace is contracted by the "dead" (703). It is natural for beast to inflict beast for survival but how do you describe the white man's (civilised) propensity to inflict pain on innocent people?

Through personification he highlights continuous peril on the world: "Again brutish necessity wipes its hands/ Upon the napkins of a dirty cause, again/ A waste of our compassion, as with Spain," (702). This reference to Spain evokes the triumph of fascism in Spain after the civil war of 1936-39. Consequently, "The gorilla wrestles with the superman." He compares the fight between the native and colonial master as "The gorilla" wrestling "with the superman". The "gorilla" becomes an extended metaphor to the "primitive" "callous" native while "superman" refers to the "refined"" civilized" colonial masters. The juxtaposition highlights the colonial discourse of binary oppositions where everything negative is ascribed to the Blackman and everything positive attributed to the whites.

What is the implication of the relationship between Africa and Britain on the persona? The poet cries out:" I who am poisoned with the blood of both, / Where shall I turn, divided into the vein?" This foregrounds the interplay of issues of history and identity that characterize Caribbean discourse generally. The hybrid nature of the Caribbean, neither/nor status. The poet is torn between two worlds and his predicament is further emphasized by "..., how choose/Between this Africa and the English tongue I love?" The poem explores and negotiates the major issue of identity which is crucial to Caribbean. It embodies the various stands of Walcott's identity --African, European and Caribbean. The complexity of this complex is echo in "Betray them both, or give back what they give?" Yet a break from either is also impossible as the poet persona laments: "How can I face such slaughter and be cool?/ How can I turn from Africa and live?" This is because of the realization of being off rooted from the African motherland and consequently the afro Caribbean identity in every respect constructed by colonization. The memory and history of this slavery impact on identity. This exemplifies the hybrid nature of the Caribbean and the persona identity is divided between Africa, Britain and Caribbean. Thus his West Indian identity is grounded both in African and British roots. Walcott creates the struggle to negotiate a kind of reconciliation between African and British identity.

While Walcott criticizes colonial history in the Caribbean, Chin Ce addresses similar issues of identity and racial awareness in Africa by presenting a picture of modern hybridized and elitist concerns of its leaders. For the Nigerian writer, the issue of whether the literary artist should or should not be concerned with what is happening in the society has through the ages been the issue over which artists and critics have debated on. Sometime during the 19th century English proponents of art-for-art's sake had held that the artists should be independent of the society and be insulated from social realities. However African literary critics have rejected this opinion and associated art with didactic and functional social criticism. Achebe had emphasized the role of the African writer as a "watchdog" of his society when he writes that "an African creative writer who tries to avoid the big social and political issues of contemporary Africa will end up being completely irrelevant" (78).

In contemporary Nigerian society, the failure of leadership and complete despair of the glamorous promises of independence have made the poets conscious of their roles as spokesmen of the people even in an artistic sense. Chin Ce, assessing the importance in African literature of his compatriot and poet, Chinweizu, also stresses the need for "cultural and artistic sensitivity in an artiste" that should "join... the bards of ancestral days in elucidating a community aesthetic" (14). Poets like Ce join the generation of young African poets who through their poetry lead the innovative discourse against the moral degeneracy of leadership in all spheres of the national and transnational human existence. Ce has been critical of Nigerian military and civilian regimes in his poetry including other aspects of leadership witnessed in Nigeria's police, educational institutions, and public bodies, Nigerian traditions, imported and hybrid religions, customs, bureaucracy, et cetera. Besides indicting the people and leaders of the continent his poetic oeuvres are often plaintive of what Irene Marques calls "the problem of artistic interpretation of these dilemmas, (in order) to imbue a sense of individual and collective meaning to the apathy and atrophy of the younger African generation" (8). In her comment on these poets who "lament the betrayal of the people's genuine aspirations for a better life", Emezue notes that "it is this form of threnody ushered by these young men that has come to be known as the new generation poetry" (126) and which, she argues, is essentially dirge in tenor. It is incontrovertible in contemporary Africa that dirge poetry as a lamentation on the occasion of death is now, due to economic and political disillusionments, a poetic exploration for leadership failures and economic mismanagement. Hence most African poets are socially conscious poets; they are steeped in the conviction that poetry is the heightened expression of life in any human society. Since their art does not exist in a vacuum, and since the society creates literature and literature, in turn, creates its society, contemporary African poets see this prescription as being vital to their critical imagination. The picture of standing social realities equally reminds listeners of ideal conditions that are open to a vivid and imaginative leadership. Thus poets in Africa see their poetry as a means of projecting human social life in the society, thereby pointing alternative ways out. This means that unless the writer is perfectly satisfied with the new society and thinks that it is ordered in the best possible way and change is not desirable, he/ she must strive to improve it through literature of commitment.

In this regard, postcolonial African poets have played a great role in the dialogue of what Chinua Achebe calls not just "a failure of leadership" (1) but "the seminal absence of intellectual rigor in the political thought of our founding fathers – a tendency to pious materialistic wooliness and self-centered pedestrianism (13). Recently African poets such as Chin Ce claim for themselves the place of traditional griot-spokesmen of their people. In the opinion of Hamilton, "Ce renders visible this legacy of colonial control as a contemporary structure of subjectification, a political system that still dominates and conditions Nigerian life, that is ripe for either revision or revolution" (108).

Chin Ce's poem "Oracle" is a call for the post colonial reengineering of African states and their cultural ethos. It is a call for greater oracular imagination against the blight of traditional and cultural amnesia. In Ce's "Oracle" Hamilton notes "the ability of the narrator (poet) to see new things, new moments of life" (114). One such instance is imagined in "the impossible detail of the 'jaws of the red ant', with all the implications of a poet-as-oracle who has the ability to regard features of the world that others pass by unwittingly" (114): "The one in the sacred grove/ Is he/ Who can see/ The jaws of the red ant" (52) declares the poet. "Divination hands/ must wash clean/ To pour the wine/ And dine with God" (52).

Ce posits a constant dialogue between past, present and future. In "Clay gods", suggestive of the idiom that the gods have clay feet, the poet wonders if the wealth of the world is one man's or a group's (gods) personal belonging. The title "Clay gods" is thus imagistic. It conjures the visionless and wanton misdirection by our "gods" (read rulers): "We had it all emblazoned/ And glistening on our black skins/ Black pride or one man's own?" (31). Here is a reflection of the contemporary society engulfed in self service and leaders who devise schemes to deny the true purpose of the commonwealth as revealed in the poem. The individualistic and opportunistic tendency of the leaders and the doom that lurks in future is replete with the image of "opiate fame" that's "filled/ The lungs and the hunter is /Ten thousand miles from home" (31). This may imply that the world is doomed because the leaders do not plan for the common good. The poet portrays the eloquence and rhetoric of the politicians with their glamorous promises in cryptic lines: "Loud bellows through the iron/ Pen" (31) which further reveals the repressive tendency of African and world leaders: "Clay gods" chronicles the inevitable results of uncommitted or insincere endeavors. The people, especially youths, in order to console themselves take to living in a state of cultural inebriation: "...and the hunter is/ Ten thousand miles from home" (31). The hint at extravagant banqueting, a main feature in the life of public leaders, fits the image of King Herod of the Christian Bible: "When again gathers/ The mob to hail/ King Herod's blasphemous feast" (31). Like Walcott who makes many Biblical references in his poems, Ce pictures the inconsistency of human nature in the public acclaim given the tyrant. The poet indifferently cautions the masses not to be carried away by myopia in the injunction: "Lose not your head in the act of fools" (31).

As a poetic experiment, the style of expression is interwoven with the thematic concern of the discourse. The effective depiction of the poet's idea (theme) depends on how he is able to manipulate his admonitory style. Emezue argues this formalistic position when she avers: "Poetry is a story that has something to be said and a way, manner, method or medium of saying it" (Mastering 3). But unlike Walcott sometimes Ce's language can be abstruse especially in "Oracle" described as an "enigmatic poem" (Hamilton 114) although such ambivalence is appropriate to the message he tries to give. In other words, the elevation of language to hidden layers of possibilities reveals the seriousness of the quest and the message it embodies. A poet expresses his thought through language even as poetry makes language a living activity. Thus when Ce, just like Walcott, queries the history and our responses to modernity in Africa with the rhetorical question in "Clay gods": "Black pride or one man's own?" (31), or when he asks in "Oracle": "Who will speak for you that fled/ Brazenly before the face of Truth?" (56), this questioning only reflects the public frustration and disillusionment that come with the degeneration and misalignment of priorities by Africa's elite intelligentsia. It must be observed, however, that the often intimate and conversational language of Ce's poetry contrasts with the indifferent and callous situation he exposes and it barely disguises the poet's derogation of public leaders. Thus the mood of Ce's poetry is rarely that of resignation as in modern African dirges which lament how postcolonial Nigerian and African leaders are merely legalized robbers acting under the protection of their constitutions. It is significant that both Derek Walcott and Chin Ce, in an ancient tradition of African literary commitment, use images and symbols to investigate and reinvigorate the historical process of identity, racial awakening and self becoming in the art of poetic evocations.

Works Cited

Achebe, Chinua. *The Trouble with Nigeria*. Enugu: Fourth Dimension Publishers, 1984.

Benítez-Rojo, Antonio. *The Repeating Island: The Caribbean and the Postmodern Perspective*. Durham and London: Duke University Press, 1996.

Ce, Chin. "A Griot of his Time: Chinweizu in Contemporary African Poetry" *African Journal of New Poetry*. No. 4, 2007 (13-31).

Ce, Chin. *An African Eclipse*. Enugu: Handel Books, 2000.

Emezue, GMT. *Comparative Studies in African Dirge Poetry*. Enugu: Handel Books, 2001.

Emezue, GMT. *Mastering Poetry*. Enugu: Handel Books,

"History of the Holocaust --An Introduction."
http://www.jewishvirtuallibrary.org/jsource/Holocaust/history.html

Fumagalli, Maria Cristina   and Peter L. Patrick.   *Two Healing Narratives: Suffering, Reintegration, and the Struggle of Language*. Small Axe 10.2 (2006) 61-79

Gikandi, Simon. *Modernism and Caribbean Literature*. Ithaca: Cornell UP, 1992.

Hogan, Linda. *Dwellings: A spiritual history of the living world*. New York: Touchstone, 1995.

Isola Akinwumi. "Limits of Tolerance: The Future of African Cultures." Nigerian National Merit Award Winner's Lecture, Calabar, Nigeria.

"Jews" Columbia Encyclopedia. http://education.yahoo.com/ reference/encyclopedia/entry?id=24532)

Marques, Irene. "Preface." *The Works of Chin Ce*. Ed. Irene Marques, IRCALC-CS(A)1, 2007.

Melas, Natalie. "Forgettable Vacations and Metaphor in Ruins Walcott's Omeros." *Callaloo* 28.1 (2005) 147-168.

Ngugi wa Thiong'o. *Decolonising the Mind: The Politics of Language in African Literature*. Oxford: James Currey, 1986.

Walcott, Derek. "A Far Cry from Africa." *An Introduction to Literature*. Sylvan Barret et al. New York: Longman, 1997:702-703.

10

Closer to Wordsworth

NATURE AND PAIN IN CHIN CE'S POETRY

Kola Eke

Few African poets have been concerned with nature and the natural world in contrast to English poets who have written much more on nature. But refreshingly in Chin Ce's poetic universe, mind and nature act and react upon each other to generate a network of pleasure and pain.

In his theme poem, "Full Moon", there is the attempt to elevate moonlighting above the ordinary pleasure of communal life. It is a poem of the mind and its relations to the external world, signified in the "moon". The description of the moonlight compels one's participation with the speaker:

> Full moon shines upon the dream
> of youth
> and wisdom may take its time
>
> The passions gather with violent
> crackling and nothing
> can stop the animated fire. (33)

The influence of nature upon him is such that the "moon" is

perceived as living. With Chin Ce, the moonlight should no longer be taken for granted, it is now gifted with passionate and energetic feelings. These very few lines show that one moment of communion with the great moods and beams of moonlight can generate enough "wisdom":

> We had met
> at crossroads, knowing not
> whence you came
> from the misty dawn of time
> to this world of violet flowers. (33)

The speaker and the moonlight as travellers run into each other. Here, "crossroads" may suggest a sense of universality. I t might be tempting to think of the poem as a dramatic monologue or lyric. There is some form of dialogue between the speaker and the moon, but this is revealed from the discourse of the single speaker:

> Your voice cut like symphony in the
> woods –
> enchanter roses among the flora:

> 'Follow me and we will search
> hidden corners of the mind
> to be joined where dread pales
> in million spectra of truth!' (34)

Although "Full Moon" is spoken by one person as he walks in the "woods" by moonlight, it does not have all the features of a dramatic monologue. For one thing, the foundation of the poem is not the revelation of the speaker's temperament but the development of his observation and feelings.

One feature, which the poem shares with the dramatic

monologue, is the single speaker who pretends to be interacting with a personified object of admiration. The poem, moreover, resembles a dramatic monologue because there is an interplay of what has been referred to as "dramatic action, an action which takes place in the present" (Byron 8). The dramatic action involves the full moon" telling the persona to "follow" to a place of rest, of revelation. Besides this action takes place in the present, so the reader becomes an observer, watching as the moon takes the speaker to a haven. The poetic haven is a place where "dread pales" in "spectra of truth". The spectroscopic imagery equates the haven to a prism, which separates the world of "dread" from happiness. In this bold picture therefore is embodied the poet's belief that nature is joy's own spectrum as this writer noted in a previous reading of Chin Ce's poetry.[1]

However, with poems such as "Prophecy", "Sweet Reminisce" and "Sail on", we begin a passage through the callous and mean countenance of nature in the poetry of Chin Ce. The poem "Prophecy" serves as this reminder that nature can be cruel too. The poet intensifies natural processes around the speaker till they seem part of his predicament:

> Somewhere on the mountain height
> and filling my puny strength
> around the slums, through the corners
> windy gusts of my breath. (13)

When these lines are considered as whole, the sense of interaction between the speaker and the landscape is quite prominent. Every detail of the setting illuminates our state of mind. Not only are the "slums" through which the speaker moves striking, they also reveal a great deal about his feelings. The "wind" blowing very hard intensifies our perception of the hardship, including the poor inhabitants of these areas, entirely depressed by their surroundings, while the stormy "wind" acts as a physical correlate to their pains. Here, the "wind" is not merely accidental; it serves a negative rather than positive purpose. The poet makes the stormy weather appropriate to the mood of his speaker:

> Around the merchant by his wares
> calling his hundred clients
> and state hounds ride the sirens
> snouts aimed at ubiquitous foes. (13)

There is a certain penetration of sadness into the poem. This is due to the cumulative impression created by the weather. One can realise the interrelationship of man and nature, showing nature as terrifying and potentially callous force. Nature is seen presenting its most sombre aspect to the speaker when he is most desolate. Apart from the speaker, nature is of no help to the petty "merchants" around the "slums". For the traders the stormy atmosphere is one of the hostile forces against which they must struggle for survival. Besides, the violence of security men is corroborated and exacerbated by a looming storm.

> Somewhere at a distant point
> gathers a mighty storm
> but only few ears shall hear
> the sound of my silent cries. (13)

Our awareness of the elements in this poem —of the climate that seems as substantial as the speaker, as well as those other poor people whose fate being depicted here— is poignant. The violent storm is a fit background to the approaching ruin that awaits victims of police brutality. Nature does intervene to make the people more uncomfortable or it is often rather cruel to their plight.

In this direction, the gathering of a "mighty storm" is the physical counterpart to the wielding of guns by the policemen. There is that same blend of mind and nature, which is characteristic of romanticism. Nature then is treated as wild and threatening, stimulating violent passions.

"Prophecy" is not the only poem in which the mood of a speaker is reflected in the natural environment. In "Sweet Reminisce", the poet, no longer interested in the physical beauty of the world around him, is now aware of its ugliness and acute estrangement of man. The poet persona gets an added sorrow from his fellowship and association with outward scenes:

> Those days were lonely moments
> Drowsing under the wooden shade
> The sun relentlessly frowned
> down on a fast scorching earth. (29)

"Sweet Reminisce" opens with the speaker remembering a period of loneliness in his life. Even though the speaker is "drowsing" under a tree, he can still feel the sterner aspect of nature. This is because of the fierce nature of sunlight. Here nature is cruel rather than loving, destructive rather than helpful, dangerous rather than friendly. From the above, one notices a transition in the movement of Chin Ce's nature poems from the preceding section where the poet thinks only of the joys of life, of the smiles of nature, of peace and tranquility. But here he recognizes the frowns of nature too. Here is a natural scene, grave to the point of melancholy, which emphasizes the speaker's mood:

> I remember how we'd stand and talk
> Till the sun had long receded
> Toward the western skies to snore
> Behind her darkened drape. (29)

This instance of anthropomorphism in Chin Ce's poetry where earlier on, the "sun" is ascribed the human quality of frowning, now has the sun gone and snoring long after the feeling of sadness and loneliness had transpired in the speaker. These lines illustrate the statement that a poet communicates meaning by sharpening and intensifying our capacity for visualization (Raghavacharyulu, 168). One captures the mental picture of a baby sleeping on its mother's back. The receding "sun" is draped around the incoming darkness of night. In this context the setting sun is the baby; while night becomes the mother.

In this painful communication, we are unhappy to share in it and sad to observe that nature frowns at him:

> Lonely moments those days; ears
> Tuned to the pulses of the night
> Moon-gazing, collapsing space,
> I had traversed the cosmic skies. (29)

Here stands a typical expression of the feelings of isolation and loneliness. Its title, "Sweet Reminisce", is therefore ironic and misleading. This is because it contains unpleasant memories. There are strong indications in the poem that natural objects such as the "sun" and "night" are intensifying the speaker's loneliness. The poem works through remembered impressions of nature.

> I'd sail all through the night
> Dreaming dreams within my heart
> How so close the beat of our souls
> Yet how so far away from reach. (29)

We are rather reminded of those moods when we are not happily related to the world around us. Chin Ce characterizes the relationship between man and nature in terms of cruelty. In his quest to find a means of conveying his "lonely" feelings, the poet looks outwards to nature for poetic emblems of the mind: the frowning sunlight and the "gazing" moon are all more than a mere correspondence; they indicate some kind of soured relationship between the internal mind and the external world. There is evidence of this in the antithesis of the last two lines where it can be noticed that the mind of man and nature are not working positively.

In "Sail On", Chin Ce displays originality and keen observation of the seascape notably in the blending description with reflection:

> I have sailed to distant lands
> By a hundred ships of war.
> I have seen deep blue hands
> Cradle the million fishes below. (14)

The poet is an authority in questions relating to the influence of external things on man. In it, the seascape is frequently portrayed as an evil influence. The poet's use of synecdoche is a great indictment of nature's callousness. It is used to emphasize that the adventurers are suffering from the biting effect of cold. Closer reading indicates that the seascape has an unpleasant influence on the speaker:

> The howling winds haunt my dreams
> Bringing echoes from distant lands
> And the lapping of the mournful waters
> Brim and drum inside my ears. (14)

Chin Ce's greatness lies in the truth and originality of his observations. The wind is blowing terribly around the crew. Apart from this, the waves are portrayed as lapping against the "ships". Moreover, the "waters" are said to be in a "mournful" mood.

Natural objects according to these lines manifest themselves in dangerous forms. As usual in Chin Ce, natural things are entirely human. Within the framework of the poem, it is his principal means of showing us nature's living hell.

The poem's last stanza emerges clearly as the cyclically unending influence of nature on human feelings:

> And the journey shall rise again
> As the sea that flow to the vast ends of space
> For the many secrets of the hidden waters
> Shall nudge the restive dreams of soul. (14)

This is an attempt to draw the speaker's spirit into the sadness evoked by his natural surroundings: the surroundings are incomplete without the mood of man through which they are reflected. With Chin Ce, nature and human mind are inseparable. This practice of drawing human realm and the realm of natural objects governs all of his poems.

CE AND WORDSWORTH

There is the constant motif in the romanticism of Chin Ce which is comparable to Wordsworth: the natural objects and the human mind upon which each poem centres. The functioning of nature and mind is for the poet the ultimate theme of poetry; in his poems the phenomenon actually receives its consummation. We notice that natural objects chiefly inhabit the scenes of most of his poems. Nature can be heard moving through the length and breadth of his poetry. Chin Ce recognizes that nature may be the source of good as well as of evil. It may excite unholy passions as well as good thoughts. In his poetry nothing in nature is dead. The poems are largely concerned with human beings as objects upon which external forces act unchecked. The poet views nature with fear and terror as often as with joy. If nature is a welcome lover, she is also a potential enemy.

Most of the poems do share certain unmistakable characteristics. One can list the various potentialities the poet finds in rocks, flowers, moonlight, sunlight and nightfall. Chin Ce feels the joy offered to us in nature and depicts it with extraordinary power in poem after poem. The poet insists in some poems that man should not be seen as a foreigner in the world of natural objects. One way in which he best achieves the happiness potentially available to him is dependent in his participation in that world.

With Chin Ce's *Full Moon* poems it has been shown that nature has its darker side too. Nature, although benevolent to man, is often hostile to the bargain. To be sure, the poet does attribute to natural objects themselves the primary quality of exciting sadness. He expressly points to nature's hostility in a good number of poems. This unity of nature's sorrowful mood to human mind is so prominent and persistent a feature of Chin Ce's poetry as to seem as much a habit of style.

Hardly any modern African poet, save Leopold Senghor of Negritude fame, has ever shown man's attachment to external objects or the soothing and scorching emotions which nature infuses in us. Ce's feeling about the natural world finds their fullest expression in the *Full Moon* poems. Often the landscape, moonscape, seascape, sunrise and sunset are an integral part of the experiences of the various speakers. They react to them with joy and sadness. These speakers are usually integrated into nature, or nature is absorbed into them.

Chin Ce therefore emerges as one African poet who in mood and temper seems closer to William Wordsworth than any other of the generation past and present. This impressive body of work makes him a significant voice and a leading poet of the new

African heritage.

NOTES

[1]For more on this idea see my earlier published paper entitled "Full Moon: The Romanticism of Chin Ce's Poetry" *Journal of New Poetry* No.4 IRCALC 2007.

WORKS CITED

Byron, Glennis. *Dramatic Monologue*. London: Routledge, Taylor and Francis, 2003.

Ce, Chin. *Full Moon*. Enugu: Handel Books, 2001.

Raghavacharyulu, D.V.K. *The Critical Response*. Madras: Macmillan, 1980.

Wordsworth, William. "Preface". *Wordsworth and Coleridge: Lyrical Ballads*. Eds. R.L. Brett and A.R. Jones. Cambridge: Univ Press, 1963. 241-272.

11

For God and Country

CHIN CE'S *MILLENNIAL*
Charles Smith

M illennial, the triad publication in Chin Ce's history of poetry writing that began since 1984[1], comes as the crystallisation of several experiences and transformations (7) involving mutual friendships that survive the heartbreaks of the millennial dawn, notes the poet. It thus appears that, in this volume, the author of *Full Moon* and *An African Eclipse* is quite prepared for what may be deemed personal – as against previous political [*African Eclipse*) or romantic (*Full Moon*) – poetry, poetry that fulfils the condition or expectation of reaching out for feelings that appeal to an individual's experience of history in the most intimate and personal details.

The history that emerged from *An African Eclipse* was one of political betrayal, public sycophancy around the circle of Nigerian military and civilian leaders and their followers. The poet had pointed accusing fingers to the failure of leadership and enjoined the people to a new awareness of the necessity of social cleansing of the land seen in Chin Ce's idea of a rebirth 'When the dirts/ In a million eyes are washed/ With clean drops of rain (58). Vigilance political or artistic is encouraged. The theme poem 'African Eclipse' came in the form of a poetic apostrophe performed by a bard singer to a Nigerian president whose politics of self promotion at the expense of public good sparked the ire of the bard-spokesman of the people. There Chin Ce acting as an African bard unequivocally rewrote the history of state terrorism against citizens and warned of possible consequences of this organized state crime. He had taken a philosophic resistance on the side of the people and brought even the landscape to disdain this despoliation of the Nigerian nation state. In strong, lamentation tones *African Eclipse* had written off political leaders of Nigeria describing them variously as treacherous reptiles that serially disenfranchise the people having systematically misappropriated public resources for their own selfish interests.

In *Full Moon* ('Dreams') the poet celebrated love and giving, longing and waiting, receiving and praising. The subject of love was likened to so many experiences through sadness and desolation, hopefulness and admiration. Love, also the privilege of missing the presence of the loved one, was above all, an eternal connection to the spirit aspect of being. In *Full Moon* Chin Ce had evoked tender feelings, given praises to heroes and the inspirers of great works in his verses, celebrated African tradition seen in his rendering of the New Yam dances of his Igbo ancestral community, and mourned nature's sometimes chaotic overflow of abundance in urban life as in a ('Suleja') storm.

Now here, in *Millennial*, poetry of deep personal significance seems to have emerged from the complex, almost mystical, interaction of the artist with his environment so simplified in Chin Ce's narratives. However, the haunting dirge tenor of most recent poetry from Africa still does not elude the poet; in fact, it is quite perceptible. Although the poems are replete with ideas of losses and disappointments in personal relationships on one hand, there exists a pervading concentration still on the relationship between citizen and nation state on the other hand. It is a relationship cast in the deep tones of disenchantment and anger in the manner of those varied "themes of political consciousness... most dominant and recurrent in contemporary Nigerian poetry" and "aimed at arousing the consciousness of the Nigerian masses to the political condition of their nation" (Onwudinjo 61-78). Chin Ce's works are therefore seamless temporal movements in the psychological order of the writer's private and public domain.

In spite of its dominant tone of dissatisfaction, *Millennial* holds a deeper and more evocative appeal towards the interpretation of individual and collective human history and experience from that "ethical principle that guarantees the manner in which we conduct ourselves" (Hamilton 104). The beginning verses commence like a journey. "I have learnt to be the fool" (12), the poet enthuses. The first is the song of the fool who must ask questions to learn new things and integrate within himself the wisdom that is never lost.

> when I know
> and never have to ask again (12)

He bids goodbye to loved ones as the journey begins, goodbyes which are also welcome exhortations:

> Even when the words
> tumble by the sides
> to stumble upon the other
> it's really no goodbye.
>
> Because our fragile hearts
> won't let go all at once

199

and we will back again
at that familiar corner of the stop. (15)

The poet's journeys are physical as well as psychological. Space
and consciousness interact remarkably on Ce's continuum of possible
meanings and rediscoveries:

A Deeper Life retreat
Takes the off turn
"Enemies are not God'
says a bread vendor (22)

...

And sooner spills the road
into Tema main
loosening the people
on tarmacs and side streets
Filling everywhere
with wares and trades. (23)

These physical spaces are mainly the West African countries of
Togo, Ghana and Benin where comparisons with the poet's own
nation-state come in subtle, humorous commentaries. The apparent
failure of Nigeria and her leaders is contrasted with the relative
success of smaller West African states.

...

This land, infinity's stretch
in brown and murky green
bring visions of a biosphere
and small, small wonders...

Rawlings was here once
His OC waves us down
for a quick-witted search
and on the journey goes. (21)

The mention of Rawlings of Ghana in the line "Rawlings was here" is probably in reference to the revolution of the former Ghanaian president which cleansed the nation of political corruption, abuse of office by men in uniform, and ensured the survival of her few indigenous industries ('Ghanacem', for instance) – something that eluded Nigeria all through the dawn of the millennium where even her own 'Nigercem' (cement manufacturing) company in eastern Nigeria had longed collapsed and been abandoned to corruption and government neglect.

> ...Ghanacem is alive
> (and selling)
> while her brother
> Nigercem is dead.
> And that was years ago! (22)

After these journeys, the poet persona in *Millennial* returns home with his usual ribaldry at the "buffoonery of the millennium" ('Bards' 23) which Nigerian politicians and their heads of state represent.

> And the fools had looked to their
> warlord
> daily as the sun was rising
> through a half and waning
> moon. (32)

This new leader of the Nigerian people is now cast in image of blood lust, a 'Hecate' with 'bloody hands'

> clawing the cross
> ...
> For more plunder of the delta
> and massacre at the mid belts. (33)

The poem, "Exile," contemplates the paradox of the logic of African nationals who flee the home state to Europe and the United States only to adopt western mannerisms and become third-rate citizens in foreign lands:

> He plunged in the waters
> of Newfoundland
> only to be bobbed on a broom
> ashore on the farther side. (29)

Finally towards the end parts, the journeys of the *Millennial* come back to the heart of the most asked philosophical question: service to self or universal good? For the poet, this service which benefits even plant life, may well be the end game of human ambitions:

> It doesn't matter
> to trim the branches
> and let in some light. (94)

Chin Ce evokes a sense of duty and friendship in very small ways that care for the environment and fauna of Africa. His sensitivity as a poet of strong ancestral memory reveals itself in this witty amalgam of short and long lines of rebuke,

> Here's the timeless cry of the
> motherless chick:
> this ground has nothing to yield;
>   the soil is purloined of truth
>   that nourished her corners. (54)

There are lines of promises and encouragement:

> Sing for me a reality

that seeks the heart
of the moment
through the universe of all
Existence…(95)

And I will wrap
my quest
in a shroud of green
leaves–

and hold your Hearts
on the softest binds
of a linen Kiss. (96)

–ending in an affirmation of universal human longing for higher awareness which had briefly marked his *Full Moon* verses: 'We will, together, / ride the crest/ of your heaven's worlds/ on and always on/ beyond this landing flight' (100).

Millennial will prove to be Chin Ce's most readable yet intensely personal poetry. It simply flows with maturity and echoes of previous sentiments while yet seeking those new "vistas of illumination" that have become the recurring framework for the interpretation or appreciation of the poet and his works.

NOTE

[1]It is possible that at least two of the three volumes of Chin Ce's poetry may have been written in the same periods. *Full Moon* is recorded as selected poems from 1984 to 1992 and, until its first publication in 2001, may have included *An African Eclipse* first published 1992. *Millennial* (2005) is described by the poet as product of "additional years of travel and sojourn" through Africa.

WORKS CITED

Ce, Chin. *An African Eclipse*. Enugu: Handel Books, 2000.

– – –. 'Bards and Tyrants: Literature, Leadership and Citizenship Issues of Modern Nigeria' *Africa Literary Journal* B5 IRCALC 2005. 3-25.

– – –. *Full Moon*. Enugu Handel Books, 1992.

– – –. *Millennial*. Enugu: Handel books. 2005

Hamilton, G. A. R. "Beyond Subjectificatory Structures: Chin Ce 'In the season of another life'" *Journal of New Poetry* (v3) IRCALC 2006. 95-117.

Onwudinjo Peter. "Political Consciousness in Contemporary Nigerian Poetry: A Study of Ada Ugah's *Naked Hearts* and *Ballads of the Unknown Soldier*." *African Literary Journal* B4 IRCALC 2003. 61-78.